TWENTIETH CENTURY VIEWS

The aim of this series is to present the best in contemporary critical opinion on major authors, providing a twentieth century perspective on their changing status in an era of profound revaluation.

Maynard Mack, *Series Editor*
Yale University

ARTHUR KOESTLER

A COLLECTION OF CRITICAL ESSAYS

Edited by
Murray A. Sperber

Prentice-Hall, Inc. A SPECTRUM BOOK *Englewood Cliffs, N.J.*

Library of Congress Cataloging in Publication Data
Main entry under title:

Arthur Koestler: a collection of critical essays.

   (Twentieth century views)   (A Spectrum Book)
   Bibliography: p.
   1. Koestler, Arthur, 1905-   —Criticism and inter-
pretation—Addresses, essays, lectures. I. Sperber,
Murray A.
PR6021.04Z569   828'.9'1209   77-7624
ISBN 0-13-049213-2
ISBN 0-13-049205-1 pbk

10   9   8   7   6   5   4   3   2   1

PRENTICE-HALL INTERNATIONAL, INC., *(London)*
PRENTICE-HALL OF AUSTRALIA PTY. LIMITED *(Sydney)*
PRENTICE-HALL OF CANADA, LTD. *(Toronto)*
PRENTICE-HALL OF INDIA PRIVATE LIMITED *(New Delhi)*
PRENTICE-HALL OF JAPAN, INC. *(Tokyo)*
PRENTICE-HALL OF SOUTHEAST ASIA PTE. LTD. *(Singapore)*
WHITEHALL BOOKS LIMITED *(Wellington, New Zealand)*

Acknowledgments

Quotations from Arthur Koestler's *The Gladiators,* American edition, are reprinted with permission of Macmillan Publishing Co., Inc. Copyright 1939 by Arthur Koestler, renewed 1967 by Edith Simon.

Quotations from Arthur Koestler's *Darkness at Noon,* American edition, are reprinted with permission of Macmillan Publishing Co., Inc. Copyright 1941 by Macmillan Publishing Co., Inc. and renewed 1969 by Mrs. F. H. K. Henrion (Daphne Hardy).

Quotations from Arthur Koestler's *Thieves in the Night,* American edition, are reprinted with permission of Macmillan Publishing Co., Inc. Copyright 1946 by Arthur Koestler, renewed 1974 by Arthur Koestler.

Quotations from Arthur Koestler's *Insight and Outlook,* American edition, are reprinted with permission of Macmillan Publishing Co., Inc. Copyright 1949 by Arthur Koestler.

My sincere acknowledgment to Arthur Koestler who has kindly given free permission to quote from the British editions of his works as well as the American editions to which he holds copyright.

For
Tom Flanagan, Ralph Rader,
and Mike Rogin,
Thanks

Contents

Introduction

by Murray A. Sperber

In the late 1930s and 1940s, with the fall of much of Europe first to the Nazis and then to the Soviets, the end of history seemed real, often imminent. In the 1950s and the early 1960s, with Cold War tension and the threat of nuclear holocaust, the apocalypse seemed equally real, in some ways more imminent. Arthur Koestler, because of his Middle European Jewish background, his refugee situation, and his personality, felt the apocalyptic nature of his times with particular intensity, and for a generation of his life, from his first book in English in 1937 to his farewell to political literature in 1955, he chose to express himself mainly in apocalyptic and prophetic modes. It is this Arthur Koestler, the author of *Darkness at Noon, The Yogi and the Commissar,* and the memoir in *The God That Failed,* as well as the speaker on the anti-Communist circuit, who is mainly remembered today.

Although Koestler earned this memory, it obscures the quality of his writing and it clouds his entire reputation. The memory, really the cliche' of the memory — Arthur-Koestler-anti-Communist — allows readers to place a dialectical and often protean writer into a very small pigeonhole. For throughout his long career, Koestler's influence has been felt on many fronts. From 1937 to 1955, he was a writer *engage',* and with Orwell, Malraux, and Silone, he represented a whole generation of politically active European authors. Since 1956, he has been immersed in questions of science and mysticism, and a large public, including many young persons, has followed his explorations. Far from being fossils of a previous age, Koestler and his work live on, and the question of his reputation — indeed, the question of the value of his work — remains open.

The rise of Koestler's reputation during the Cold War, and its subsequent decline, is in part the result of his success in speaking for a very large public. *Spanish Testament* (1937), a polemic and memoir about the Spanish Civil War, was hailed by readers and critics because its mood confirmed their own sense of the times. Left Book Club audiences in Britain applauded the author on tour; George Orwell, in his review of the book, particularly agreed with Koestler's apocalyptic refrain, "Europe is lost."[1] Again, in 1941, readers and critics welcomed *Darkness at Noon* as much for its apparent answer to "The Riddle of Moscow's Trials"—the title of the front-page *New York Times Book Review* piece[2]—as for its literary merits. Throughout the '40s, a time of mass social and political dislocation, Koestler's memoirs and fiction seemed to many British and American readers to describe not only the plight of the displaced person, but also the human condition. During World War II, it was said of him: "Mr. Koestler, who was simply a leftist a few years ago, belongs to the new youth and is a forerunner prophetic in stature of the men who will come home from the war."[3]

When Koestler turned his prophetic talent to anti-Communism, many readers were willing to follow and others to join. In *The Yogi and the Commissar* (1945), one of the first Cold War tracts, he managed to articulate widely held fears and beliefs. When, in 1950 and 1951, hundreds of thousands of readers felt similarly enlightened by his memoir in *The God That Failed* and enthusiastic audiences viewed the stage adaptation of *Darkness at Noon,* he was regarded as a culture hero, the creator of literary works that spoke to the conscious and unconscious wishes of a society.

In the middle '50s, however, ever restless, as well as wary, as if anticipating both the eventual decline of the Cold War and the waning of his own prophetic powers, Koestler declared his political-literary period over. In the preface to *Trail of the Dinosaur* (1955) he wrote: "...I have said all that I had to say on these questions which had obsessed me, in various ways, for the best part of a quarter of a century. Now the errors are atoned for, the bitter passion has burnt itself out; Cassandra has gone hoarse, and is due for a vocational change." Since this pronouncement, he has written mainly

---

[1] George Orwell, review of *Spanish Testament* by Arthur Koestler, *Time and Tide,* February 5, 1938, p. 67.

[2] Harold Strauss, "The Riddle of Moscow's Trials," *New York Times Book Review,* May 25, 1941, pp. 1, 18.

[3] H. A. Reinhold, review of *Arrival and Departure* by Arthur Koestler, *Commonweal,* December 24, 1943, pp. 255-56.

about science and mysticism, and although on occasion he has returned to fiction, essays, and history, the literary works have been *divertissements* from the major scientific projects. His inquiries into the nature of artistic creation, culminating in *The Act of Creation* (1964), have won him a large international audience as well as official honors—he is now a Commander of the British Empire. Yet he has never regained the prominence in European and American intellectual life that he had during his literary-political phase.

According to a recent interview, Koestler feels that his scientific work has been slighted and that it, not his literary-political writing, will be remembered in future years.[4] This position is understandable; but in denying his earlier works—for example, he calls the memoirs "cold vomit"—he also denies the positive response that they elicited (and still do) from large numbers of readers as well as some of the best literary and political commentators. My purpose in this collection of essays, therefore, is not only to assemble the best that has been written about Koestler but to inquire into the permanent value of his work. If critics treated his writing with too much seriousness in the '40s and '50s, their subsequent neglect seems just as unfounded. In the post-Cold War climate, it should be possible to look at all of Koestler's writing, sort out the valuable from the ephemeral, ascertain why he still speaks to and for so many readers, and, finally, ask what if any claims on posterity his work has.

II

Koestler's critics can be divided into three groups: "participants," who, during the Cold War especially, share with Koestler his various moods, particularly the apocalyptic; "analysts," who, more critical than the participants, nevertheless respond deeply to his writing and offer clues and insights into his work; and "censurers," who are entirely out of sympathy and thus immune to Koestler's powers and any real understanding of his achievement.

Although the participant critics point to and help elaborate the emotional power of Koestler's writing, they never disengage themselves from it to view it in perspective—they simply react to its psychological and political signals. During the Cold War, leftists,

[4]George Feifer, "A Conversation with Arthur Koestler," *Saturday Review,* March 6, 1976, p. 23.

rightists, and establishment liberals often responded with equal ardor. Even certain writers who turned against him, like Kingsley Martin, the editor of the *New Stateman,* never really stepped out of the Koestlerian frame. Following the Cold War, many science writers joined the participants: Koestler's positions on scientific questions being contentious and almost always controversial, he has attracted large numbers of scientific partisans and opponents, who argue about his work in a most unscientific way.

Most participant writing is unreadable today. Since neither Koestler's nor their own apocalypses came to pass, the political participants seem frozen within the '40s and '50s. Even the scientific participants, especially those reacting to Koestler's prophecies of genetic disaster, seem frozen within the '60s. For this reason, I have excluded this group of critics from the collection. (For a vivid and extended sample of their work, see the book reviews and articles on Koestler in *Time* magazine and *Commonweal* in the 1940s and early 1950s.)

The work of the second group of Koestler critics, the analysts, began to appear in the early '40s, mainly in *Partisan Review, New Republic,* and *New Statesman.* Well versed in Freudian and Marxist thought, most of these writers were able to identify the psychological and political problems in Koestler's work and avoid participation in them. The group included Philip Rahv, William Phillips, Diana Trilling, Isaac Rosenfeld, Harold Rosenberg, and Saul Bellow (all members of the 1940s' New York literary scene); another group, independently sharing many of the same concerns about politics and literature, in general, and Koestler, in particular, included Edmund Wilson, F. O. Matthiessen, Malcolm Cowley, Stephen Spender, Isaac Deutscher, George Woodcock, and George Orwell, who like Koestler, was at one time a "Letter from London" writer for *Partisan Review.* Unfortunately, the majority of these critics dropped Koestler, probably because of his Cold War activities, in the late '40s. This collection returns to print many of their best pieces. Today, it is among science and philosophy writers that the analytic approach seems most alive. Essays, reprinted here, by Henry David Aiken, Stuart Hampshire, George Steiner, and Stephen Toulmin explicate Koestler's thought and work dispassionately and place it within European intellectual history.

A total lack of sympathy for Koestler defines the third group of critics. The censurers do not form a chorus or antichorus like the participants, and they do not consider the psychopolitical elements in Koestler's work like the analysts. They do, however, challenge or censure his performance from various positions, especially traditional aesthetic ones, and in so doing sometimes make useful points about it. Unfortunately, they usually argue from narrow premises: the aesthetic critic assumes an eternal split between politics and literature, and the chauvinist critic dismisses Koestler's work because he is not a native. Raymond Mortimer gives the gist of all such positions when he claims that Koestler "is not English" (every *Times Literary Supplement* review of Koestler's work during the 1940s contained some version of this complaint), "not a novelist" (the main problem for V. S. Pritchett through five book reviews and one long essay, reprinted here), and "as a writer, [not] even likable."[5] Many science and philosophy writers also belong to the censurers, viewing Koestler's recent work with the same quiet superiority.

III

In this collection of essays, I have divided the selections according to the two main subject areas of Koestler's career, politics/literature, and science/mysticism. Within each division I have ordered the selections, with one minor exception, chronologically. In this way, I hope to give the reader some sense of the events and controversies that affected Koestler's writing and usually his critics' responses.

In the reception of Koestler's first book in English, *Spanish Testament* (1937), one review stands out: George Orwell's short piece in *Time and Tide*. Orwell, although not well known in 1937 and earning a precarious income from book reviewing, immediately championed *Spanish Testament* and pointed out the quality of Koestler's imagination.

Over the next few years, Orwell reviewed the novels *Darkness at Noon* and *Arrival and Departure* as they appeared, but, in 1944, apparently not satisfied with his understanding of Koestler's work, he

---

[5] Raymond Mortimer, "Arthur Koestler," *Cornhill Magazine* (Winter 1946); 213-22.

wrote a long essay on the subject. He begins by defining Koestler's place in English literature as well as the qualities that separate him from the English tradition. Then, working through the fiction, he uncovers and defines "the nightmare atmosphere which is, so to speak, his patent" and which was to influence his own *Animal Farm* and *1984*. Orwell's article offers not only a clear assessment of Koestler's writing and politics, especially in terms of their '30s and '40s frame of reference, but sheds light on the evolution of Orwell's own work.

Malcolm Cowley also reviewed Koestler's early books and then returned for a retrospective essay. His account of *Darkness at Noon* seems too generous to the official Soviet line on the Moscow Purge Trials, but his biographical connection of Koestler and Rubashov, the novel's hero, remains more suggestive than almost all of the subsequent commentary on the subject. As with Cowley, so with others. Because Koestler's writing did not fit into conventional categories, he forced the best critics into reexamining their ideas about literature. Saul Bellow, Harold Rosenberg, F. O. Matthiessen, and Edmund Wilson offer definitions of his work in which his immediately recollected memoirs and scarcely fictional novels are central. Much of Koestler's early as well as best writing, especially *Dialogue with Death* and *Scum of the Earth* (F. O. Matthiessen's favorite), anticipates the nonfiction novel and life-as-tract so popular today.

Throughout the 1940s, Koestler lived amidst controversy. *Thieves in the Night* (1946), particularly Koestler's endorsement of Zionist terrorist tactics in Palestine, precipitated a nasty debate among British and American intellectuals. Of the many contributions to this debate (see also the pieces by Philip Rahv and Diana Trilling listed in the Selected Bibliography), Isaac Rosenfeld's piece is particularly acute, both in its specific analysis of Koestler's argument and its general description of his strengths and weaknesses.

When *Darkness at Noon* was first published in Paris in 1946, it was immediately caught up in the great postwar debate between Communists and Republicans over who was to govern France. Adding to the heat of the occasion was the author himself, who lived part time in France during these years and answered all attacks in kind. (See Simone de Beauvoir's *The Mandarins* for an undisguised portrait of Koestler at this time.) Maurice Merleau-Ponty wrote in

Humanism and Terror—his chapter (see p. 75), "Koestler's Dilemmas," is reproduced here—that Koestler had totally failed to understand Marxism and the nature of revolution. Merleau-Ponty argues dialectically, within the Marxist-Hegelian tradition, and his condemnation of Rubashov—"Finally, *once he has been arrested,* Rubashov the opposition menber *becomes* in truth a traitor" (Merleau-Ponty's emphasis)—is both illuminating and frightening. Merleau-Ponty is able to show us *Darkness at Noon* from a position far more complex than that of Anglo-American "New Criticism," but he reveals attitudes and arguments, and ways of arguing, that are too close to Stalinism to attract many Western readers.

Rebecca West's British commonsensical approach to Communism and especially Communists contrasts with Merleau-Ponty's theoretical and abstract one. She focuses on the human drama in Koestler's short memoir in *The God That Failed* and finds it a "subtle and candid and comprehensive statement" of a "typical experience of this age." With one exception, in 1950, all critics of this work agreed with West's evaluation. Only Isaac Deutscher, an ex-member of the Polish Communist party, saw Koestler's statement as unsubtle, uncandid, uncomprehensive, and his experience as untypical. Deutscher's advantage over other critics is his authentic knowledge of Communism from within; thus when he questions Koestler's credentials, he makes a series of telling points. In my own article, "Looking Back on Koestler's Spanish War," I raise a similar but more specific point about the autobiographies: Koestler's later versions of his Spanish Civil War experiences contradict his earlier memoirs on the subject, and the differences—unacknowledged by the author—indicate important changes in his politics, personality, and literary skills.

In 1949, Koestler broke away from his political concerns with his first book on science, *Insight and Outlook: An Inquiry into the Common Foundations of Science, Art, and Social Ethics.* Many of his political supporters were baffled by this excursion into scientific and philosophical speculation. Koestler, however, had merely returned to one of his earliest loves (he had been a science student at the University of Vienna and later a science writer in pre-Nazi Germany). Although he would not commit himself entirely to science for a number of years, *Insight and Outlook* seems in retrospect less the aberration that it appeared to reviewers at the time and more a foreshadowing of things to come.

In his review of the book, A. J. Ayer, the Oxford philosopher, treated Koestler as he might a bright undergraduate who has "discovered" an all-comprehensive philosophy. The *Scientific American* critic, James R. Newman, examined Koestler's "bisociated" theory of conflict more seriously (he even reproduced a number of the book's diagrams), but concluded that Koestler's ideas were "a vague, grandiose, metaphor-ridden *Welt Philosophie* which smells a little of Hegel, Spengler and Freud." No critic pointed out that Koestler's emphasis on the collision of opposites with resulting synthesis— his "bisociation" theory—was analogous to his obsession with political dialectic and apocalyptic vision.

After the 1949 work, Koestler waited ten years before publishing another book on science. Then, within a decade, he brought out a major trilogy, *The Sleepwalkers: A History of Man's Changing Vision of the Universe* (1959), *The Act of Creation* (1964), and *The Ghost in the Machine* (1968), as well as collections of essays. *The Sleepwalkers* was generally well received by critics. Stuart Hampshire, among others, praises Koestler's powers of narration and explication, although he has reservations about the originality of Koestler's thought. George Steiner, in his review of *The Act of Creation,* emphathizes with the author, his background, and the polymath nature of his career, explicating the book from within and then managing to step aside and place it in terms of contemporary science writing. Henry David Aiken's approach to *The Act of Creation* is more philosophical: after explaining (and resisting) Koestler's thesis, he concludes that Koestler is neither a scientist nor a novelist but a traditional metaphysician. Again, however, no critic paused to consider Koestler's science and mysticism as elements of autobiography, part of a lifelong narrative of the self. William Empson, in a review of the volume of essays, *The Lotus and the Robot* (1961), mentions the restless nature of Koestler's personality and his habit of moving from one faith to another; and Leslie Fielder, in a review of the final volume of the science trilogy, claims that the "ghost" of *The Ghost in the Machine* is the author himself, the science being merely a cover for Koestler's quarrel with the '60s.

But these interesting suggestions are dropped as soon as made. Of all of the areas of Koestler's work, the autobiographical is the most ignored and the most in need of serious study.

Stephen Toulmin in a major essay, "The Book of Arthur," places a historical frame around Koestler's thought and work. Toulmin locates Koestler's science within the tradition of German philosophy and shows the origins of his often disparate theories. The essay is so exhaustive in its delineation of Koestler's scientific ideas that it seems the perfect piece with which to conclude this collection.

Undoubtedly, the most striking tribute to Arthur Koestler is the range of critics needed to analyze his work. They include, or should include, literary critics, political writers and theorists, natural scientists, philosophers, psychologists, and students of religion. No single writer so far has been able to focus on more than one or two areas of Koestler's work. It will require all of them, working at or near the top of their powers and complementing each other, to complete the labor of review and appraisal whose beginnings are commemorated in these pages.

Review of *Spanish Testament*

by George Orwell

Mr. Arthur Koestler, a *News Chronicle* correspondent, stayed in Malaga when the Republican troops had departed—a bold thing to do for he had already published a book containing some very unfriendly remarks about General Queipo de Llano. He was thrown into jail by the rebels, and suffered what must have been the fate of literally tens of thousands of political prisoners in Spain. That is to say, he was condemned to death without trial and then kept in prison for months, much of the time in solitary confinement, listening at his keyhole night after night for the roar of rifle-fire as his fellow-prisoners were shot in batches of six or a dozen. As usual—for it really does seem to be quite usual—he knew that he was under sentence of death without knowing with any certainty what he was accused of.

The prison part of the book is written mainly in the form of a diary. It is of the greatest psychological interest—probably one of the most honest and unusual documents that have been produced by the Spanish war. The earlier part is more ordinary and in places even looks rather as though it had been "edited" for the benefit of the Left Book Club. Even more than Mr Steer's,[1] this book lays bare the central evil of modern war—the fact that, as Nietzsche puts it, "he who fights against dragons becomes a dragon himself."

Mr Koestler says:

> I can no longer pretend to be objective....Anyone who has lived
> through the hell of Madrid with his eyes, his nerves, his heart, his

"Review of *Spanish Testament* by Arthur Koestler," by George Orwell. From *Time and Tide* (February 5, 1938), 67. Reprinted in *Collected Essays, Journalism, and Letters of George Orwell*, Volume I, edited by Sonia Orwell and Ian Angus, copyright © 1968 by Sonia Brownell Orwell. Reprinted by permission of Harcourt Brace Jovanovich, Inc., and Secker & Warburg Co., Ltd.

[1] *The Tree of Gernika* by G. L. Steer.

stomach—and then pretends to be objective, is a liar. If those who have at their command printing machines and printer's ink for the expression of their opinions, remain neutral and objective in the face of such bestiality, then Europe is lost.

I quite agree. You cannot be objective about an aerial torpedo. And the horror we feel of these things has led to this conclusion: if someone drops a bomb on your mother, go and drop two bombs on his mother. The only apparent alternatives are to smash dwelling houses to powder, blow out human entrails and burn holes in children with lumps of thermite, or to be enslaved by people who are more ready to do these things than you are yourself; as yet no one has suggested a practicable way out.

Arthur Koestler

by George Orwell

One striking fact about English literature during the present century is the extent to which it has been dominated by foreigners — for example, Conrad, Henry James, Shaw, Joyce, Yeats, Pound and Eliot. Still, if you chose to make this a matter of national prestige and examine our achievement in the various branches of literature, you would find that England made a fairly good showing until you came to what may be roughly described as political writing, or pamphleteering. I mean by this the special class of literature that has arisen out of the European political struggle since the rise of Fascism. Under this heading novels, autobiographies, books of "reportage," sociological treatises and plain pamphlets can all be lumped together, all of them having a common origin and to a great extent the same emotional atmosphere.

Some out of the outstanding figures in this school of writers are Silone, Malraux, Salvemini, Borkenau, Victor Serge and Koestler himself. Some of these are imaginative writers, some not, but they are all alike in that they are trying to write contemporary history, but *unofficial* history, the kind that is ignored in the text-books and lied about in the newspapers. Also they are all alike in being continental Europeans. It may be an exaggeration, but it cannot be a very great one, to say that whenever a book dealing with totalitarianism appears in this country, and still seems worth reading six months after publication, it is a book translated from some foreign language. English writers, over the past dozen years, have poured forth an enormous spate of political literature, but they have produced almost nothing of aesthetic value, and very little of historical value

"Arthur Koestler" by George Orwell [written 1944]. From *Dickens, Dali, and Others,* 1946. Reprinted in *Collected Essays, Journalism, and Letters of George Orwell,* Volume III, edited by Sonia Orwell and Ian Angus, copyright © 1968 by Sonia Brownell Orwell. Reprinted by permission of Harcourt Brace Jovanovich, Inc., and Secker & Warburg Co., Ltd.

either. The Left Book Club, for instance, has been running ever
since 1936. How many of its chosen volumes can you even remember
the names of? Nazi Germany, Soviet Russia, Spain, Abyssinia,
Austria, Czechoslovakia—all that these and kindred subjects have
produced, in England, are slick books of reportage, dishonest
pamphlets in which propaganda is swallowed whole and then spewed
up again, half digested, and a very few reliable guide books and text-
books. There has been nothing resembling, for instance, *Fontamara*
or *Darkness at Noon,* because there is almost no English writer to
whom it has happened to see totalitarianism from the inside. In
Europe, during the past decade and more, things have been happening to middle-class people which in England do not even happen to
the working class. Most of the European writers I mentioned above,
and scores of others like them, have been obliged to break the law
in order to engage in politics at all; some of them have thrown
bombs and fought in street battles, many have been in prison or the
concentration camp, or fled across frontiers with false names and
forged passports. One cannot imagine, say, Professor Laski in-
dulging in activities of that kind. England is lacking, therefore, in
what one might call concentration-camp literature. The special
world created by secret-police forces, censorship of opinion, torture
and frame-up trials is, of course, known about and to some extent
disapproved of, but it has made very little emotional impact. One
result of this is that there exists in England almost no literature of
disillusionment about the Soviet Union. There is the attitude of
ignorant disapproval, and there is the attitude of uncritical admiration, but very little in between. Opinion on the Moscow sabotage
trials, for instance, was divided, but divided chiefly on the question
of whether the accused were guilty. Few people were able to see
that, whether justified or not, the trials were an unspeakable horror.
And English disapproval of the Nazi outrages has also been an unreal thing, turned on and off like a tap according to political ex-
pediency. To understand such things one has to be able to imagine
oneself as the victim, and for an Englishman to write *Darkness at
Noon* would be as unlikely an accident as for a slave-trader to write
Uncle Tom's Cabin.

  Koestler's published work really centres about the Moscow trials.
His main theme is the decadence of revolutions owing to the corrupt-

ing effects of power, but the special nature of the Stalin dictatorship has driven him back into a position not far removed from pessimistic Conservatism. I do not know how many books he has written in all. He is a Hungarian whose earlier books were written in German, and five books have been published in England: *Spanish Testament, The Gladiators, Darkness at Noon, Scum of the Earth,* and *Arrival and Departure.* The subject-matter of all of them is similar, and none of them ever escapes for more than a few pages from the atmosphere of nightmare. Of the five books, the action of three takes place entirely or almost entirely in prison.

In the opening months of the Spanish civil war Koestler was the *News Chronicle*'s correspondent in Spain, and early in 1937 he was taken prisoner when the Fascists captured Malaga. He was nearly shot out of hand, then spent some months imprisoned in a fortress, listening every night to the roar of rifle fire as batch after batch of Republicans was executed, and being most of the time in acute danger of execution himself. This was not a chance adventure which "might have happened to anybody," but was in accordance with Koestler's life-style. A politically indifferent person would not have been in Spain at that date, a more cautious observer would have got out of Malaga before the Fascists arrived, and a British or American newspaper man would have been treated with more consideration. The book that Koestler wrote about this, *Spanish Testament,* has remarkable passages, but apart from the scrappiness that is usual in a book of reportage, it is definitely false in places. In the prison scenes Koestler successfully establishes the nightmare atmosphere which is, so to speak, his patent, but the rest of the book is too much coloured by the Popular Front orthodoxy of the time. One or two passages even look as though they had been doctored for the purposes of the Left Book Club. At that time Koestler still was, or recently had been, a member of the Communist Party, and the complex politics of the civil war made it impossible for any Communist to write honestly about the internal struggle on the Government side. The sin of nearly all left-wingers from 1933 onwards is that they have wanted to be anti-Fascist without being anti-totalitarian. In 1937 Koestler already knew this, but did not feel free to say so. He came much nearer to saying it—indeed, he did say it, though he put on a mask to do so—in his next book, *The Gladiators,* which was published about a year before the war and for some reason attracted very little attention.

The Gladiators is in some ways an unsatisfactory book. It is about Spartacus, the Thracian gladiator who raised a slaves' rebellion in Italy round about 65 BC, and any book on such a subject is handicapped by challenging comparison with *Salammbô*. In our own age it would not be possible to write a book like *Salammbô* even if one had the talent. The great thing about *Salammbô*, even more important than its physical detail, is its utter mercilessness. Flaubert could think himself into the stony cruelty of antiquity, because in the mid-nineteenth century one still had peace of mind. One had time to travel in the past. Nowadays the present and the future are too terrifying to be escaped from, and if one bothers with history it is in order to find modern meanings there. Koestler makes Spartacus into an allegorical figure, a primitive version of the proletarian dictator. Whereas Flaubert has been able, by a prolonged effort of the imagination, to make his mercenaries truly pre-Christian, Spartacus is a modern man dressed up. But this might not matter if Koestler were fully aware of what his allegory means. Revolutions always go wrong—that is the main theme. It is on the question of *why* they go wrong that he falters, and his uncertainty enters into the story and makes the central figures enigmatic and unreal.

For several years the rebellious slaves are uniformly successful. Their numbers swell to a hundred thousand, they overrun great areas of Southern Italy, they defeat one punitive expedition after another, they ally themselves with the pirates who at that time were the masters of the Mediterranean, and finally they set to work to build a city of their own, to be named the City of the Sun. In this city human beings are to be free and equal, and above all, they are to be happy: no slavery, no hunger, no injustice, no floggings, no executions. It is the dream of a just society which seems to haunt the human imagination ineradicably and in all ages, whether it is called the Kingdom of Heaven or the classless society, or whether it is thought of as a Golden Age which once existed in the past and from which we have degenerated. Needless to say, the slaves fail to achieve it. No sooner have they formed themselves into a community than their way of life turns out to be as unjust, laborious and fear-ridden as any other. Even the cross, symbol of slavery, has to be revived for the punishment of malefactors. The turning-point comes when Spartacus finds himself obliged to crucify twenty of his oldest and most faithful followers. After that the City of the Sun is doomed, the slaves split up and are defeated in detail, the last fifteen thousand of them being captured and crucified in one batch.

The serious weakness of this story is that the motives of Spartacus himself are never made clear. The Roman lawyer Fulvius, who joins the rebellion and acts as its chronicler, sets forth the familiar dilemma of ends and means. You can achieve nothing unless you are willing to use force and cunning, but in using them you pervert your original aims. Spartacus, however, is not represented as power hungry, nor, on the other hand, as a visionary. He is driven onwards by some obscure force which he does not understand, and he is frequently in two minds as to whether it would not be better to throw up the whole adventure and flee to Alexandria while the going is good. The slaves' republic is in any case wrecked rather by hedonism than by the struggle for power. The slaves are discontented with their liberty because they still have to work, and the final break-up happens because the more turbulent and less civilised slaves, chiefly Gauls and Germans, continue to behave like bandits after the republic has been established. This may be a true account of events—naturally we know very little about the slave rebellions of antiquity—but by allowing the Sun City to be destroyed because Crixus the Gaul cannot be prevented from looting and raping, Koestler has faltered between allegory and history. If Spartacus is the prototype of the modern revolutionary—and obviously he is intended as that—he should have gone astray because of the impossibility of combining power with righteousness. As it is, he is an almost passive figure, acted upon rather than acting, and at times not convincing. The story partly fails because the central problem of revolution has been avoided or, at least, has not been solved.

It is again avoided in a subtler way in the next book, Koestler's masterpiece, *Darkness at Noon.* Here, however, the story is not spoiled, because it deals with individuals and its interest is psychological. It is an episode picked out from a background that does not have to be questioned. *Darkness at Noon* describes the imprisonment and death of an Old Bolshevik, Rubashov, who first denies and ultimately confesses to crimes which he is well aware he has not committed. The grown-upness, the lack of surprise or denunciation, the pity and irony with which the story is told, show the advantage, when one is handling a theme of this kind, of being a European. The book reaches the stature of tragedy, whereas an English or American writer could at most have made it into a polemical tract. Koestler has digested his material and can treat it on the aesthetic level. At the same time his handling of it has a political implication, not important in this case but likely to be damaging in later books.

Naturally the whole book centres round one question: Why did Rubashov confess? He is not guilty—that is, not guilty of anything except the essential crime of disliking the Stalin regime. The concrete acts of treason in which he is supposed to have engaged are all imaginary. He has not even been tortured, or not very severely. He is worn down by solitude, toothache, lack of tobacco, bright lights glaring in his eyes, and continuous questioning, but these in themselves would not be enough to overcome a hardened revolutionary. The Nazis have previously done worse to him without breaking his spirit. The confessions obtained in the Russian state trials are capable of three explanations:

1. That the accused were guilty.

2. That they were tortured, and perhaps blackmailed by threats to relatives and friends.

3. That they were actuated by despair, mental bankruptcy and the habit of loyalty to the Party.

For Koestler's purpose in *Darkness at Noon* 1 is ruled out, and though this is not the place to discuss the Russian purges, I must add that what little verifiable evidence there is suggests that the trials of the Bolsheviks were frame-ups. If one assumes that the accused were not guilty—at any rate, not guilty of the particular things they confessed to—then 2 is the common-sense explanation. Koestler, however, plumps for 3, which is also accepted by the Trotskyist Boris Souvarine, in his pamphlet *Cauchemar en URSS*. Rubashov ultimately confesses because he cannot find in his own mind any reason for not doing so. Justice and objective truth have long ceased to have any meaning for him. For decades he has been simply the creature of the Party, and what the Party now demands is that he shall confess to non-existent crimes. In the end, though he had to be bullied and weakened first, he is somewhat proud of his decision to confess. He feels superior to the poor Czarist officer who inhabits the next cell and who talks to Rubashov by tapping on the wall. The Czarist officer is shocked when he learns that Rubashov intends to capitulate. As he sees it from his "bourgeois" angle, everyone ought to stick to his guns, even a Bolshevik. Honour, he says, consists in doing what you think right. "Honour is to be useful without fuss," Rubashov taps back; and he reflects with a certain satisfaction that he is tapping with his pince-nez while the other, the relic of the past, is tapping with a monocle. Like Bukharin, Rubashov is "looking out upon black darkness." What is there, what code, what loyalty, what notion of good and evil, for the sake of which he can defy the Party and endure further torment? He is not only alone, he is also hollow. He has himself committed worse crimes than the one that is now being perpetrated against him. For example, as a secret envoy of the Party in Nazi Germany, he has got rid of disobedient followers by betraying them to the Gestapo. Curiously enough, if he has any inner strength to draw upon, it is the memories of his boyhood when he was the son of a landowner. The last thing he remembers, when he is shot from behind, is the leaves of poplar trees on his father's estate. Rubashov belongs to the older generation of Bolsheviks that was largely wiped out in the purges. He is aware of art and literature, and of the world outside Russia. He contrasts sharply with Gletkin, the young GPU man who conducts his interrogation, and who is the typical "good party man," completely without scruples or curiosity, a thinking gramophone. Rubashov, unlike Gletkin, does not have the Revolution as his starting-point. His mind was not a blank sheet when the Party got hold of it. His superiority to the other is finally traceable to his bourgeois origin.

One cannot, I think, argue that *Darkness at Noon* is simply a story dealing with the adventures of an imaginary individual. Clearly it is a political book, founded on history and offering an interpretation of disputed events. Rubashov might be called Trotsky, Bukharin, Rakovsky or some other relatively civilised figure among the Old Bolsheviks. If one writes about the Moscow trials one must answer the question, "Why did the accused confess?" and which answer one makes is a political decision. Koestler answers, in effect, "Because these people had been rotted by the Revolution which they served," and in doing so he comes near to claiming that revolutions are of their nature bad. If one assumes that the accused in the

Moscow trials were made t. confess by means of some kind of ter
rorism, one is only saying that one particular set of revolutionary
leaders has gone astray. Individuals, and not the situation, are to
blame. The implication of Koestler's book, however, is that Rubashov
in power would be no better than Gletkin: or rather, only better in
that his outlook is still partly pre-revolutionary. Revolution, Koestler seems to say, is a corrupting process. Really enter into the Revolution and you must end up as either Rubashov or Gletkin. It is
not merely that "power corrupts": so also do the ways of attaining
power. Therefore, all efforts to regenerate society *by violent means*
lead to the cellars of the OGPU, Lenin leads to Stalin, and would
have come to resemble Stalin if he had happened to survive.

Of course, Koestler does not say this quite explicitly, and perhaps
is not altogether conscious of it. He is writing about darkness, but
it is darkness at what ought to be noon. Part of the time he feels that
things might have turned out differently. The notion that so-and-so
has "betrayed," that things have only gone wrong because of individual wickedness, is ever present in left-wing thought. Later, in
Arrival and Departure, Koestler swings over much further towards
the anti-revolutionary position, but in between these two books there
is another, *Scum of the Earth*, which is straight autobiography and
has only an indirect bearing upon the problems raised by *Darkness
at Noon*. True to his life-style, Koestler was caught in France by the
outbreak of war and, as a foreigner and a known anti-Fascist, was
promptly arrested and interned by the Daladier Government. He
spent the first nine months of war mostly in a prison camp, then,
during the collapse of France, escaped and travelled by devious
routes to England, where he was once again thrown into prison as
an enemy alien. This time he was soon released, however. The book
is a valuable piece of reportage, and together with a few other scraps
of honest writing that happened to be produced at the time of the
débâcle, it is a reminder of the depths that bourgeois democracy
can descend to. At this moment, with France newly liberated and the
witch-hunt after collaborators in full swing, we are apt to forget that
in 1940 various observers on the spot considered that about forty
per cent of the French population was either actively pro-German
or completely apathetic. Truthful war books are never acceptable to
non-combatants, and Koestler's book did not have a very good

reception. Nobody came well out of it—neither the bourgeois politicians, whose idea of conducting an anti-Fascist war was to jail every left-winger they could lay their hands on, nor the French Communists, who were effectively pro-Nazi and did their best to sabotage the French war effort, nor the common people, who were just as likely to follow mountebanks like Doriot as responsible leaders. Koestler records some fantastic conversations with fellow victims in the concentration camp, and adds that till then, like most middle-class Socialists and Communists, he had never made contact with real proletarians, only with the educated minority. He draws the pessimistic conclusion: "Without education of the masses, no social progress; without social progress, no education of the masses." In *Scum of the Earth* Koestler ceases to idealise the common people. He has abandoned Stalinism, but he is not a Trotskyist either. This is the book's real link with *Arrival and Departure,* in which what is normally called a revolutionary outlook is dropped, perhaps for good.

Arrival and Departure is not a satisfactory book. The pretence that it is a novel is very thin; in effect it is a tract purporting to show that revolutionary creeds are rationalisations of neurotic impulses. With all too neat a symmetry, the book begins and ends with the same action—a leap into a foreign country. A young ex-Communist who has made his escape from Hungary jumps ashore in Portugal, where he hopes to enter the service of Britain, at that time the only power fighting against Germany. His enthusiasm is somewhat cooled by the fact that the British Consulate is uninterested in him and almost ignores him for a period of several months, during which his money runs out and other astuter refugees escape to America. He is successively tempted by the World in the form of a Nazi propagandist, the Flesh in the form of a French girl, and—after a nervous breakdown—the Devil in the form of a psychoanalyst. The psychoanalyst drags out of him the fact that his revolutionary enthusiasm is not founded on any real belief in historical necessity, but on a morbid guilt complex arising from an attempt in early childhood to blind his baby brother. By the time that he gets an opportunity of serving the Allies he has lost all reason for wanting to do so, and he is on the point of leaving for America when his irrational impulses seize hold of him again. In practice he cannot abandon the struggle. When the book ends, he is floating down in a parachute over the dark landscape of his native country, where he will be employed as a secret agent of Britain.

As a political statement (and the book is not much more), this is insufficient. Of course it is true in many cases, and it may be true in all cases, that revolutionary activity is the result of personal mal-adjustment. Those who struggle against society are, on the whole, those who have reason to dislike it, and normal healthy people are no more attracted by violence and illegality than they are by war. The young Nazi in *Arrival and Departure* makes the penetrating remark that one can see what is wrong with the left-wing movement by the ugliness of its women. But after all, this does not invalidate the Socialist case. Actions have results, irrespective of their motives. Marx's ultimate motives may well have been envy and spite, but this does not prove that his conclusions were false. In making the hero of *Arrival and Departure* take his final decision from a mere instinct not to shirk action and danger, Koestler is making him suffer a sud-den loss of intelligence. With such a history as he has behind him, he would be able to see that certain things have to be done, whether our reasons for doing them are "good" or "bad." History has to move in a certain direction, even if it has to be pushed that way by neu-rotics. In *Arrival and Departure* Peter's idols are overthrown one after the other. The Russian Revolution has degenerated, Britain, symbolised by the aged consul with gouty fingers, is no better, the international class-conscious proletariat is a myth. But the con-clusion (since, after all, Koestler and his hero "support" the war) ought to be that getting rid of Hitler is still a worth-while objective, a necessary bit of scavenging in which motives are almost irrelevant.

To take a rational political decision one must have a picture of the future. At present Koestler seems to have none, or rather to have two which cancel out. As an ultimate objective he believes in the Earthly Paradise, the Sun State which the gladiators set out to establish, and which has haunted the imagination of Socialists, Anarchists and religious heretics for hundreds of years. But his intelligence tells him that the Earthly Paradise is receding into the far distance and that what is actually ahead of us is bloodshed, tyranny and privation. Recently he described himself as a "short-term pessimist." Every kind of horror is blowing up over the horizc n, but somehow it will all come right in the end. This outlook is probably gaining ground among thinking people: it results from the very great difficulty, once one has abandoned orthodox religious belief, of accepting life on earth as inherently miserable, and on the other hand, from the realisation that to make life liveable is a much bigger problem than it recently seemed. Since about 1930 the world has given no reason for optimism whatever. Nothing is in sight except a welter of lies, hatred, cruelty and ignorance, and beyond our present troubles loom vaster ones which are only now entering into the European consciousness. It is quite possible that man's major problems will *never* be solved. But it is also unthinkable! Who is there who dares to look at the world of today and say to himself, "It will always be like this: even in a million years it cannot get appreciably better"? So you get the quasi-mystical belief that for the present there is no remedy, all political action is useless, but that somewhere in space and time human life will cease to be the miserable brutish thing it now is.

The only easy way out is that of the religious believer, who regards this life merely as a preparation for the next. But few thinking people now believe in life after death, and the number of those who do is probably diminishing. The Christian churches would probably not survive on their own merits if their economic basis were destroyed. The real problem is how to restore the religious attitude while accepting death as final. Men can only be happy when they do not assume that the object of life is happiness. It is most unlikely, however, that Koestler would accept this. There is a well-marked hedonistic strain in his writings, and his failure to find a political position after breaking with Stalinism is a result of this.

The Russian Revolution, the central event in Koestler's life, started out with high hopes. We forget these things now, but a quarter of a century ago it was confidently expected that the Russian Revolution would lead to Utopia. Obviously this has not happened. Koestler is too acute not to see this, and too sensitive not to remember the original objective. Moreover, from his European angle he can see such things as purges and mass deportations for what they are; he is not, like Shaw or Laski, looking at them through the wrong end of the telescope. Therefore he draws the conclusion: This is what revolutions lead to. There is nothing for it except to be a "short-term pessimist," i.e. to keep out of politics, make a sort of oasis within which you and your friends can remain sane, and hope that somehow things will be better in a hundred years. At the basis of this lies his hedonism, which leads him to think of the Earthly Paradise as desirable. Perhaps, however, whether desirable or not, it isn't possible. Perhaps some degree of suffering is ineradicable from human life, perhaps the choice before man is always a choice of evils, perhaps even the aim of Socialism is not to make the world perfect but to make it better. All revolutions are failures, but they are not all the same failure. It is his unwillingness to admit this that has led Koestler's mind temporarily into a blind alley and that makes *Arrival and Departure* seem shallow compared with the earlier books.

Koestler: The Disenchanted

by Malcolm Cowley

When Malaga was lost in the early spring of 1937, Arthur Koestler fell into the hands of the Rebels. He had once met Queipo de Llano, the Rebel general; he had even published an interview telling the truth about him, and that was crime enough to condemn a journalist. Without being tried, he was sentenced to death.

That spring, Koestler was thirty-one years old. He was a Hungarian subject, an exile from Germany and a roving correspondent for *The News Chronicle,* the bravest paper in London. For the last six years he had been a Communist Party member; he had spent some time in Moscow and had traveled through Central Asia as a guest of the Soviet government. He had also finished his first novel, which was a curious book for any Communist to have written.

The Gladiators, which would not be published in this country [i.e., the United States] until 1939, was a novel purporting to deal with Spartacus and the Servile War. Its main outlines were indeed historical, but it was full of anachronisms that seemed to be deliberate—as if Koestler was saying that he didn't care when Lucullus returned from the East or what the Roman slaves were given to eat; one year or another, horse beans or maize, it was all the same to him, because he wasn't really writing about the Romans. His real subject was not one particular revolt against Roman landlords beginning in 73 B.C., but all the revolts in recorded history. He was, moreover, telling a fable for our own times, in which one could recognize familiar people and topics—Anarchists, Trotskyists, party liners, deviations, the end justifying the means. Spartacus himself was presented, not as a Thracian gladiator, but rather as a combination of Lenin in Smolny

"Koestler: The Disenchanted," by Malcolm Cowley. From *The New Republic,* 107 (July 20, 1942), 89-90. Copyright 1942 by *The New Republic;* copyright renewal 1970 by Malcolm Cowley. Reprinted by permission of the author.

Institute and Christ on the cross. It was of course permissible for any
Communist to discuss the reasons why his revolt was a failure, but
Koestler went far beyond political issues or historical events. Pain-
fully, awkwardly, shifting his attention from one character to another as if afraid of coming to the point, he managed to imply—as
if against his will—that every revolution must be abortive or betrayed and that any revolutionary leader, after becoming a dictator
by the logic of his position, must end by destroying those he is fighting to save.

Thus, Koestler in Malaga had been sentenced to die for a cause
that he had already begun to question. During the hundred days
when he was waiting to face a firing squad—first in Malaga and then
in Seville—he felt no sense of solidarity with his fellow prisoners
as a group; in more senses than one, he was kept in solitary
confinement.

The story of his Spanish adventures appeared in England the following year; it was called *Spanish Testament.* A shorter version,
omitting all the chapters that dealt with the war in general and including only his personal experiences, has just been published here
under the new title of *Dialogue with Death.* It is not the greatest
prison narrative even of our own times, but it is among the easiest
to read. Whereas *The Gladiators* was technically an apprentice work,
Dialogue with Death has the characteristics of Koestler's mature
writing: the gift for straightforward narrative, the taste for intro-
spection, the observations on human nature—often full of wisdom—
the interest in moral issues, which leads him to pass severe judge-
ments on himself, and finally the air of complete candor with which
he tells his own story. "The main difficulty," he says in a foreword,
"was the temptation to cut a good figure"; and this is an especially
great temptation to men playing even a minor part in politics, since
they assume that any reflection on themselves would also be a reflection on the party to which they belong. Koestler, by avoiding it—
by presenting himself as a quite unheroic but living figure—managed
to write a book that is no less moving today than it was when we still
hoped for victory in Spain.

After his release from prison—which he owed partly to his friends
in England and partly to a series of accidents involving the Hearst
newspapers and a collection of filthy postcards—Koestler had a
moral crisis. He resigned from the Communist Party and began

writing a novel about the Moscow trials; it would not be finished until a few weeks before the fall of France. Meanwhile he had been having a series of adventures that would be the subject of another autobiographical work. He had been arrested by the French police and had spent the winter in the concentration camp at Le Vernet, which in most respects was worse than the German camp at Dachau. Released by the intervention of his English friends, he had returned to Paris, where he lived under constant threat of being sent back to prison, and yet was never told the nature of the charges against him. Then, after the German invasion, he had escaped to the south, enlisted in the Foreign Legion, and finally made his way to England. All these adventures are described in *Scum of the Earth,* which is the most personal, the most eloquent and apparently the most exact of all the narratives dealing with the fall of France.

As for the novel that he finished and sent to the printer at almost the last possible moment—a few days later and it would have been seized with his other manuscripts by the French police—it was later published here as *Darkness at Noon.* Though it deals with the Russian trials, it obviously contains elements borrowed from Koestler's own story. Thus, most of the Russian characters are composite portraits of Communists he knew. The prison he describes so graphically is like no building that ever stood in Moscow; it actually resembles the Model Prison in Seville. The men who pass his hero's cell on the way to execution were condemned to death by Franco, not by Stalin. And Koestler was able to write his convincing account of a prisoner examined by the Gaypayoo because, at the moment of writing, he was himself being persecuted by the French political police. Throughout the book he is blaming Russia for the sins of her opponents; though he would answer this statement—and not without good reasons on his side—by saying that all dictatorships are forced to use the same methods, whatever their ultimate goals may be. He is, however, unfair to the Russians in other ways as well. Writing in the bitterness of personal disillusionment, and in the conviction that Stalin had become Hitler's faithful ally, he makes points and presses home accusations which, I imagine, he would now like to withdraw.

But although *Darkness at Noon* is not a safe guide to contemporary politics, and although much of its force as a pamphlet was destroyed when Hitler crossed the Russian border, it has other values that make it worth rereading. Its real theme is not the wickedness of the Russian dictatorship, but rather the everlasting conflict between the political universe and the moral universe. In developing this theme, the author leads us to deeper and deeper psychological levels, as if we were being guided downwards through a series of caves. At first we believe—and Rubashov the hero believes—that he is an innocent man about to be executed for crimes of which he was absolutely incapable. Then, going deeper into his own case, he is forced by the examining magistrates to admit that he is guilty by the Communist standards he has always proclaimed. Groping still deeper into his mind, he decides to reject Communist standards, but that is no solution; judged by the older principles of Christian ethics, his conduct has been even more deserving of punishment. Rubashov's explorations of his own personality are cut short by a pistol shot, but the reader gets a hint of further depths, especially if he is familiar with Koestler's two autobiographical works. It seems clear enough that the hero represents the author; that in this book Koestler is symbolically standing trial before his own conscience, is confessing the errors of his past life as a Communist, and is himself being led to execution in the cellars of the Lubyanka Prison. *Darkness at Noon* is a powerful work of fiction partly because it is, for its author, a ritual of sacrifice and atonement.

But it is also important because it stands for the literature of a new period. During the six or eight years before the Spanish civil war, the mood of the younger writers had been Utopian and even apocalyptic. They thought that bourgeois society would soon be destroyed, but they hoped—and many of them believed with a deep religious feeling—that a happier world would be erected on its ruins by a process somewhat resembling the Russian five-year plans. André Malraux was the great new figure of this period, finding new symbols to express its faith in the future. The hero of *Man's Fate*, waiting to be burned alive with two hundred other Communists after the suppression of the revolt in Shanghai, has no fear whatever of dying. "He had fought for what in his time was charged with the deepest meaning and the greatest hope; he was dying among those with whom he would have wanted to live; he was dying, like each of these men, because he had given a meaning to his life. What would have been the value of a life for which he would not have been willing to die? It is easy to die when one does not die alone." Malraux's novel about the Spanish war was even more confident, although this time the mood seemed a little forced. Its title in English was *Man's Hope* and in French simply *L'Espoir*.

By the time it was published, however, most of the hopefulness had vanished. In the new period that was beginning in literature as well as politics, the prevailing mood would be one of defeat and disenchantment. It is not a mood or a time that makes writing easy, and the new period has not yet produced any novelists of Malraux's stature. Koestler is a lesser figure, but so far he has been its most effective spokesman. And the death of Rubashov, in *Darkness at Noon*, forms a curious contrast with the death of Malraux's hero, as if a century had intervened. Rubashov is dying for a faith in which he no longer believes. What he discovers while waiting for the end is not a sense of comradeship, but rather the feeling of individuality that he had lost during his political career. As the guard leads him into the cellars of the Lubyanka, he reflects that "it was easy to die with the visible certainty of one's goal before one's eyes. He, Nicholas Salmanovich Rubashov, had not been taken to the top of a mountain; and wherever his eye looked, he saw nothing but desert and the darkness of night."

A Revolutionist's Testament

by Saul Bellow

Whatever single criticisms may be made of him, Arthur Koestler is one of the very few living novelists who attacks the most difficult and troubling issues of private and political morality and who, having raised serious questions, never tries to satisfy us with ready-made answers or evasions.

In the deepest and most real sense, *Arrival and Departure* — like the earlier *Dialogue With Death* and *Darkness at Noon* — is a war book; not only because its hero escapes from a Fascist country to wear, in the end, a British uniform, but because his choice involves full awareness of the individual and collective problems posed by the war for this generation. Koestler speaks from the authority of his own experience. As a Hungarian-born correspondent for a British newspaper during the Spanish Civil War he was captured and sentenced to death; since his escape he has fought with both the French and the British armies; now, at 38, he is in England working for the British Broadcasting Company.

The hero of his preceding novel, *Darkness at Noon,* was Rubashov, a former People's Commissar who decided to testify falsely at a public trial against himself and other old Bolsheviki. "History has taught us that often lies serve her better than truth," he wrote in his prison journal. And also, "As the only moral criterion which we recognize is that of social utility, the public disavowal of one's convictions in order to remain in the Party's ranks is obviously more honorable than the quixotism of carrying on a hopeless struggle." Schooled in this kind of reasoning, he was convinced that he was making a necessary sacrifice. Or partly convinced; for he gradually became aware that he was wasting himself; his cause was

"A Revolutionist's Testament," by Saul Bellow. From *The New York Times Book Review* (November 21, 1943), 1, 53. © 1943 by The New York Times Company. Reprinted by permission.

irretrievably lost. There was neither "social utility" nor utility of any other sort in his dying, but to live in the state he had helped create was also impossible. And so, with regret and with cynicism and dread, he went. It was as much his devotion to a certain ideal of reason as the executioner's bullet that killed Rubashov.

Arrival and Departure takes for its subject the effect on morality of another ideal of reason. This time Koestler raises the following questions: When we have succeeded in understanding what it is in the growth of our minds, our early histories, that drives us to serve causes, is it then proper for us to abandon those causes? What if it is proved to us that our hunger for justice is a sign of neurosis, are we absolved from our responsibility for justice? Is it a sign of health to seek satisfaction for one's self and of morbidity to recognize an obligation to ethical values?

It is with these questions that the refugee Peter Slavek is concerned. Despite his youth—he is only 22—he is a disillusioned veteran of revolutionary politics.

In his homeland he has already become a legendary hero: he refused to give information to the Fascists even though they offered him every inducement of broken bones and burning cigars extinguished on his body. In Neutralia, the country to which he has escaped, he plans to enlist (with the British, apparently; the sides are not specifically named) against the enemy. He is far too well educated politically to make an uncritical choice. He sees the three belligerents as a triangle. "One side was utopia betrayed; the second tradition decayed; the third destruction arrayed." It is, of course, necessary to oppose destruction "but it was a duty, not a mission."

When, however, Peter is confronted with the alternatives of joining "tradition decayed" or going to America, he falls ill and for a time his right leg, which had been burned by his torturers, is paralyzed. He is treated by a psychoanalyst, Dr. Sonia Bolgar, and, as she skillfully confesses him in a darkened room, the hero who would give no information to the Fascists becomes by his own account a child expiating his early guilt. His cause was the just one; that of the Fascists unjust. He knew that. And yet their police represented authority and their torturers in the bare basement room became for him a priesthood of fathers. They, for their part, understood the necessity for reducing their victim to childishness, making him ashamed of his body, humiliated at its natural functions. But, fouled and bleeding, he nevertheless did not give them what they wanted, he refused to turn informer.

Peter is well aware that Utopia has been betrayed; he no longer cares about the Movement. But what interests Dr. Bolgar is his original reason for joining it. At home he had been an upper-class intellectual. Why had he rejected safety and courted punishment? The answer which Dr. Bolgar finds as she pushes him back toward the beginnings of his conscience is that he desired martyrdom and had welcomed punishment. And the reason for his desire was that he was convinced he had "betrayed" everyone — peasants, workers, a group of Jews whose execution he had been forced to witness, his mother. He had begun in earliest childhood by "betraying" a rabbit called Jerusalem, linked in Peter's mind with the psalm, "If I forget thee, O Jerusalem, may my right hand lose its cunning." The victim was unwittingly eaten. But his ghost obscures an even greater crime committed by Peter against his younger brother, a spoiled child whom he hated.

These things having been made clear, Dr. Bolgar begins to free Peter from the net of errors in which his leg is caught. A worldly, hard-minded woman, she represents a different ideal of reason than Rubashov's. She is the scientist of the wish and of the unconscious racial memory. To her, convictions, values, causes, are "mere pretexts of the mind, phantoms of a more intimate reality," history is no more than a "chain of accidents." As for prophets and crusaders, they try to deny the true ends of life; the enemies they strike at are within them, they strike blindly, hunting themselves. They are false to their own deepest needs. Hence they are stigmatized. "They try to hide it," she says, "by being doctrinaire, or matter of fact and tough, but when they are alone and naked they sweat little drops of blood through their skin."

Peter now regains the use of his leg. Obviously, his next move is to save himself, to go to America. But he is not wholly convinced by Dr. Bolgar; he is unable to feel that all his life is contained in his nerves and memories. He has inherited a morality as well as a "racial unconscious," and if this ethical compulsion of his is a sickness then all human societies are held together by sickness, by irrational faith, by a need, perhaps morbid and self-destructive, to pay their moral debts.

Rubashov, awaiting death in his cell, repudiated the whole course along which his reason had led him and reflected: "Perhaps it did not suit man to be completely free from old bonds." Peter, too, rejects the advice of reason and obeys instead the advice of feeling. He decides to remain in Europe and fight.

Mr. Koestler has given *Arrival and Departure* the full benefit of his marvelous ability to create a contemporary atmosphere and to make his characters represent the whole of the civilization to which they belong. But he has made his opponent, Dr. Bolgar's ideal of reason, a little too easy to refute. Dr. Bolgar is not the best representative of her type as Rubashov is of his. He is a perfect old Bolshevik. She, however, is too obvious; a priestess of some psychoanalytic cult, single-mindedly serving the native, sinless, unashamed instincts. The character of moral judgments may have been changed by modern psychology, but moral judgments themselves have not been abolished nor the need for them disclaimed.

But at all events, Peter, in making his choice, admits that Sonia Bolgar is, so far as logic goes, in the right. However, faith has its own requirements, despite logic. And perhaps "in these spheres the right thing [has] always to be done for the wrong reasons." There is no science of moral convictions, that, in effect, is what Koestler is saying. By themselves, our ideals of reason mean very little; they have brought us few benefits and done us great damage. Perhaps in the next age civilization will turn again to the problems of ethical belief, abandoned since the Renaissance for the problems of experimental science. Then all mankind may join in answering the questions of moral choice which individual men today attack with inadequate means and at the risk of their lives.

The Case of the Baffled Radical

by Harold Rosenberg

A new literature seems to have made its appearance — the literature of conscience of the ex-Communist.

Primarily a movement among journalists, the literary abnegation of "The Party" has already produced some outstanding novels, notably Ignazio Silone's *Bread and Wine* and Arthur Koestler's *Darkness at Noon.*

This literature of the Communist backslider has little in common with the epics of Party conversion known as "proletarian" writing a decade ago. The dramas of Bolshevik piety drew their main thinking, naturally, from the organization into which the initiate was delivering himself. In contrast, the work of the de-converted Red belongs to the main stream of modern writing; it is part of the tradition of doubt and negation which has occupied first place in literature for the past 100 years. Upon the Communist precepts and practices Koestler lets loose the disintegrating machinery of skepticism, ambivalence and psychiatry — weapons of the type used by Joyce in assaulting Catholic education, by Mann against the ethics of middle-class duty, or by Gide against the accepted morality of personal relations.

Measured by the accomplishment of the masters of the past generation both the art and the skepticism of Koestler are quite thin. But as one of the best chroniclers of the moral Flight From Moscow, he brings to the novel something new or long-neglected — political sophistication and a serious sense of the human drama of public events. Koestler understands how modern man is defeated in the conference rooms and the daily press, on the battlefields and in the dungeons of Europe. He is aware of viciousness and weakness not only, as the older writers knew it, as something inherent — he knows

"The Case of the Baffled Radical," by Harold Rosenberg. From *Partisan Review*, XI (Winter 1944), 100-103. Copyright January 1944 by *Partisan Review*; renewed October 1971. Reprinted by permission of the author.

it also as something *made,* even *made* "according to plan." ... Perhaps the task of the artist today is rendered more difficult by the increased brutality of our culture; he is forced to deal with new problems and areas of data from which his art, as such, will gain nothing—just as the soldier at the front finds it harder to keep alive though the quality of his life is not raised by these difficulties.

Koestler's *Arrival and Departure* is the story of the education of Peter Slavek, fugitive ex-Communist, in the dubious sources of his own revolutionary heroism. Upon his arrival in "Neutralia" (there ought to be a law against such place-names), with which the book begins, Peter has already given up his connection with The Party, after many months in a Nazi concentration camp. Why? Because the very intensity of the sufferings he had borne without cracking had helped to convince this 22-year old son of the middle class that his resistance was due to some other source than loyalty to the Party. The rank-and-file Party members had succumbed to the tortures of the Gestapo and had betrayed their oath, and they admired this faithful Peter as a hero. But isn't there something suspicious, Peter asked himself, in being a hero?

Yet when he jumps ship at Neutralia, Peter is still a carrier of banners, determined to get back into the battle through offering himself as a volunteer to the British. While waiting, however, for the slow processes of the Consulate to lift him out of neutrality, he falls in love with a French refugee, Odette, a girl whose moral philosophy is neatly summed up by Koestler in the phrase, "After all—why not?"

The love affair, which Koestler handles rather spottily, ends abruptly when Odette leaves without warning for America. The sudden abandonment proves too much for Peter; he is smitten with a psychic paralysis of the right leg, on which the Nazi torturers have left fatal stigmata of cigar burns. The most exciting sequence in the novel is the unexpected physical collapse of Peter as the scar of the burn in the bend of his knee becomes a hole through which "the strength had run out of his leg like water out of the bath of Sonia," the female psychoanalyst in whose apartment he is staying.

The core of the book is the psychic analysis itself, during which the half-allegorical figure of Dr. Sonia Bolgar rocks in her chair by the bedside of the fallen warrior, drawing from him the tale of his deeds and his dreams. The surface layers of Peter's mental tissue contain the horrors of his actual experiences in Nazi Europe—his capture, the black-clad torturers, the "mixed transports" in which captured girls, gypsies and Jews are dragged across the continent to nightmarish fates. But when these memory fabrics are torn up by the analysis, they bring with them, like an uprooted sod, growths belonging to still deeper fears and defeats: childhood crimes, expiations and vows to which all his adult life has chained itself through symbolic transferences and confusions of identity. When the bottom is reached, and the original sin disinterred—the "accidental" putting out of his brother's eye at the age of five, which he knew subconsciously was not an accident at all—Peter is cured, "cured of his illusions, both about objective aims and subjective motives."

The new Peter decides to cast aside all political totems—"What real good had come of those quixotic crusades?" But a certain uneasiness springs up in connection with this plan too. However disillusioned he may have become, Peter is dedicated to political action, "he is not the type to back out and cultivate a garden." Below the values uprooted by psychoanalysis, judgments continue to form themselves, perhaps simply out of the need to act, characteristic of Peter and his generation.

The final episodes of *Arrival and Departure* indicate clearly the poles of Koestler's thinking—they are the same as those that appear in the works of Thomas Mann and a good deal of other modern literature. On the one hand, the road of a relaxed yielding to events, cessation of struggle, and personal self-indulgence (identified with love): "After all—why not?" On the other, a leap in the direction of "duty," duty *felt,* not arrived at by reason and even opposed to reason: "Here we go" is the phrase Koestler uses as a key.

"Don't you think," the shot-up British flier asks Peter, "that it's rather a boring game trying to find out one's reasons for doing something?"

Thus, as Castorp in *The Magic Mountain* is last seen advancing across No Man's Land, the baffled Peter reaches action and even consciousness of possessing moral values when he leaps out over enemy country in a parachute. At the last moment, he had quitted the ship that was to take him to America and the immoral Odette— since duty is better than giving way. And he had made the final discovery that reasons are a thing of the past, for we live at the end of the age of science and "a new god is about to be born." "Here we go," trusting ourselves happily to the void in the cradle of a parachute; perhaps out of this act of self-abandonment the future diety will take shape.

Because of the intelligence, and particularly the *relevance,* of his novels, it is easier to praise Koestler than to indicate the correct proportion of his lack. His thinking tackles boldly some of the most real dramatic situations of our time. And it never forgets the personal sufferings of those who are caught in them. At the same time there is a pervading glibness in Koestler, the journalist satisfying himself with devices aimed at the reader's opinions. This glibness is not altogether a vice, since it permits the author to put down quickly and cleanly events whose meanings a more painstaking investigation might not reveal for a long time or might even find to be out of reach entirely. Haste is especially important for the chronicler of political conscience, since the background of the drama changes so rapidly today that details of doubt recorded about, say, Spain in 1935 no longer have the same point if described in 1943.

But for the readiness of his formulas, Koestler pays a high price. For instance, his handling of the psychoanalytical process is extremely well planned, but the quality of the symbols is uneven; some are subtly selected personal images, others are text-book clichés. The writing, too, is marred by easily acquired phrases and ideas: phrases like "another symbolic toy which he had hung on the Christmas tree of his guilt"; ideas like the theatrical notion of Peter that he has the duty to save mankind and that at the time of the Flood "there should have been at least one who ran back into the rain, to perish with those who had no planks under their feet."

Also, for all its philosophical fashionableness, the conclusion of *Arrival and Departure,* with its assertion of the *necessary* failure of the modern mind in the face of historical problems and its call for a new deity, is intellectually gross. For the book has not even raised the problem of socialism versus fascism which it pretends to exhaust. It does not criticise the particular political philosophy of Peter—he might as well have been a heroic Protestant minister. It merely argues that heroism is always the result of infantile guilt feelings, that the political always violates the personal, and that any reasoned political action involving sacrifices is therefore always wholly neurotic.

The notion that psychoanalysis gives plausibility to these conclusions is extremely superficial. The analysis is shown to have destroyed Peter's ability to make a judgment of fascism, whereas, actually, by removing his dream interpretation of the enemy, analysis should have deepened his consciousness of what fascism means. Koestler has all but left himself in the position of trying to demonstrate the contradiction that without neurotic compulsions man cannot behave intelligently.

Koestler approaches politics with a fixed philosophical dualism that distorts his understanding of the tragedy of the left intellectual of the past decade. In *Darkness at Noon,* also a novel of atonement, he did not attack the jailers of Rubashov for specific violations of socialist values, but placed the responsibility on Rubashov himself as representing with them a metaphysical absolute—"the logic of history"—opposed to the individual by the nature of things. The effect of this mechanical dichotomy (which also appears in Koestler's essays) was to cause Rubashov, introduced as one of the revolutionary founders of the USSR, to conceive his political life as nothing more than a series of crimes against the individual—it was the guilt he incurred in "representing history" that he expiated in confessing at the trial. Such a criticism of The Trials is a metaphysical not a political or historical criticism, and in effect it accepts the political and historical claims of the Communists while rejecting their moral ones.

But without concrete politics, no concrete political characters. Unlike Silone, whose fascists are living types, Koestler's novels of guilt talk about characters more often than they reveal them dramatically. The scene between Peter and Radich, Chief of the Political Department, is a marvellous dramatic opportunity—utterly missed. The same is true of Koestler's Communists; they remain invisible behind their "ideas."

No doubt the ex-Communists are baffled in the face of the present world situation. Koestler's prophecy that "a new god is about to be born" has no other content than this bafflement. The new god is a religious or mythological device which fills his hero with serene enthusiasm by ending his need to understand what is taking place. In this shape confusion is positive and homeopathic. The trouble is that it makes "Here we go" identical with "After all—why not?" and political action into a sexual experience.

The Essays of Arthur Koestler

by F. O. Matthiessen

These essays[1] by Arthur Koestler possess a particular value for
Americans, since we have no equivalent for him in this country. A
man of 40, of Hungarian birth and a journalist by profession, he
has lived through all the phases of the long battle against fascism
in a way that our fortunate detachment has spared us from doing.
A correspondent in the Soviet Union in the early Nineteen Thirties,
he was for some years a member of the Communist party, but broke
with it at the time of the Moscow trials. A representative for a London paper in Spain during the civil war, he was imprisoned and
narrowly escaped execution at the hands of Franco. At the outbreak
of the present war he was in Paris, and suffered the ironic fate of
many other anti-Fascist "foreigners" by being sentenced to the concentration camp at Le Vernet. Released just in time to witness the
fall of France, he managed to escape to the south and eventually to
England. The best of his books so far, *Scum of the Earth,* records
that year's experience unforgettably. His chief novels, *Darkness
at Noon* and *Arrival and Departure,* convey respectively his disillusion with the Russian Revolution and his probing examination
of the European state of mind in its defensive stand against fascism.

His collection of essays all date within the past four years, and
reveal his deepening preoccupations. He surveys the role of "the
intelligentsia" from the era of the French Revolution, and believes
in its responsibility to preserve the "aspiration to independent
thinking." During the past decade of savage persecutions, when men
of thought have had to wage a rear-guard battle and often to de-

"The Essays of Arthur Koestler," by F. O. Matthiessen. From *The New York
Times Book Review* (May 27, 1945), 1, 21. © 1945 by The New York Times Company. Reprinted by permission.

[1][*The Yogi and the Commissar and Other Essays* (New York: Macmillan & Co.,
1945). — Ed.].

ploy on narrow and narrower margins, he has held to the duty of independence—"in a world where nobody is well: *the duty not to accept.*" He functions at his best when he makes us see the Atlantic gulf that separates those who have known the European convulsion at first hand from those who have not. Requested by *The New York Times Magazine* to write an article, "based on personal experience, on what gives men faith to fight to the end for the democratic way," he responded early in 1943 with "Knights in Rusty Armor." He told there the kind of truths that we do not now like to hear, such as that "the nearer victory comes in sight, the clearer the character of the war reveals itself as what the Tories always said it was—a war for national survival, a war in defense of certain conservative nineteenth-century ideals, and not what I and my friends of the Left said that it was—a revolutionary civil war in Europe on the Spanish pattern."

In his tribute to Richard Hillary, a talented beginning novelist who gave his life as a pilot in the RAF, Koestler probes farther the issue of "fighting faith." Hillary was intensely conscious of belonging to the new Lost Generation, "disillusioned and spoiled," whose brief lives spanned only between wars. Koestler makes a significant counterpoint between an Oxford don's letter of condolence to the pilot's father, recalling Dick's "indomitable spirit" as stroke of his college crew in 1939, and Hillary's own analysis of how he and his university contemporaries attacked "the middle-class society to which they owe their education and position," and yet failed to make any effectual contact with "the practical exponents of labor." He felt that they were balancing precariously between "a despised world they had come out of and a despising world they couldn't get into" —a feeling shared by many of their American middle-class counterparts. But as soon as war was declared, Hillary enlisted and was one of the group who saved his country in the Battle of Britain. Yet he was impelled to write his novel, *The Last Enemy,* because he got "so sick of the sop about 'The Knights of the Air'" that he had to say that it was "in spite of" that sop and "not because of it" that "we still felt this war worth fighting."

In "The Fraternity of Pessimists" Koestler formulates his own somber confession of faith, that "in this war we are fighting against a total lie in the name of a half-truth." He sees in our victory no lasting solution for the minority problems in Europe, and no cure "for the inherent disease of the capitalistic system." He casts a doubting glance at America's future handling of racialism, since he believes that fascism is the same whether in Warsaw, Calcutta, or Detroit. He is only made uneasy by the Hollywood version of the heroic sergeant on Bataan who "seems always apt to confound Abraham Lincoln with President Harding." At a time when we would like to think this the last war, Koestler looks ominously ahead. He believes that "the only asset left on a bankrupt continent" is in the men of action and sensitivity in the resistance movements, those "pioneers in the fight to safeguard the dignity of man."

Koestler is not an original, nor a particularly powerful, thinker. Rather he is a man of acute feeling who has suffered long and intensely. He knows that suffering alone does not produce wisdom; and yet the great dividing line now is "between those who have suffered and those who have remained relatively untouched." Consequently, his chief service is that he enables us to penetrate beyond that line by observing what the experience of our time has done to a representative European intellectual. Only against his background can we understand his attitude toward the two symbols of his title. For he now feels compelled to formulate human behavior at its two extremes. At the infra-red extreme he sees the Commissar, who believes in Change from Without and that the End justifies the Means. At the ultra-violet extreme he sees the Yogi, who believes in Change from Within, that "the End is unpredictable and that the Means alone count." They have no common meeting ground. The one is concerned with the individual's relation to society, the other with his relation to the universe.

It must be observed that such symbols are very literary, and that Koestler's thinking is often imaginatively rich at the expense of strict logical coherence. But the main interest is to perceive how he arrived at these symbols, and why a man with his strong political concerns now feels that he is travelling consciously, if unwillingly, toward the ultra-violet end.

The answer lies in his longest essay, "Soviet Myth and Reality," in which he discusses "the end of an illusion." Other reviewers with more detailed knowledge of the U.S.S.R. will debate the significance of many of his excoriating charges. Suffice it to say here that his argument is that Russia is moving away from rather than toward socialism. He finds, to be sure, that her economic structure is "historically progressive" compared with the capitalist economy of other countries, but that "in every other respect," socially and culturally, she is "regressive," and often brutally so. It is interesting to note the mixed conclusions to which this argument leads him. He declares that he is still a Socialist, and that the failure of the Russian experiment against the backward and reactionary background of czarism "neither proves nor disproves the possibility of socialism." Yet he says in another essay that if he had to choose between living under a Commissar or a Blimp, he would "unhesitatingly choose Blimp." And yet again he recognizes that the only aim of "the conservative position" is "to maintain somehow the *status quo,* ...to counter dynamism by inertia. It holds no promise for the victors and has no plan for the vanquished."

Koestler is most symptomatic of recent history in the degree to which he has made politics a substitute for religion. He knows now that the Soviet Union he yearned for was a myth. But he still seems insufficiently aware of the reasons for his disillusion. He made such impossible demands for an immediate utopia that his dreams inevitably turned into a nightmare. Others who have expected less from Russia will give more weight than Koestler does to her economic advance within a single generation. And looking ahead to the increasing interplay between Russia and the rest of the world during the next generation, they will not speak as though the Stalinist state must remain an unchanging iron-age.

The most salutary lesson Koestler has learned is "that economic factors are important, but not all-important," that there is more to human history than nineteenth-century materialism conceived. He is now suspicious also of the shallow optimism that stemmed from the eighteenth-century Enlightenment, of its ignoring of the dark irrational forces in man. He believes that we have to recover what religion taught: "that there are two ways of knowing: *exploration* of the horizontal, worldly planes, and *contemplation* of the vertical or transcendental order."

But in reaching that position he appears now upon the verge of another mistake, as disastrous as was his perfectionist's demand upon politics. He is so much the uprooted intellectual that he seems to have no religious tradition to which to turn, and has to take refuge in a vague personal mysticism. He sees through such oddities as the yoga of a Gerald Heard, yet apparently believes that methods of contemplation survive only in Oriental philosophy. He seems to forget the implications of what Richard Hillary wrote to the fellow-pilot he admired most: "In an age when to love one's country is vulgar, to love God archaic, and to love mankind sentimental, you do all three."

It may be one of the real assets of being an American now that we don't need to feel so uprooted and without an effectual past. If we want enough to recover the force of religious truth and the transforming power of love, we can find them through our own inheritance from Europe. "That all men are created equal" was a political formulation, but it took for granted the background of Christian ethics. Our most profound social affirmations, as in Lincoln's Emancipation Proclamation, are both political and religious. And it is equally striking that the strongest renewal in our theology today is through such a figure as Reinhold Niebuhr, who is concerned with both Christianity and democracy, with the individual's relation to society as well as to the universe.

The evidence is the same in our imaginative expression. Our creative writers of the nineteenth-century who impress us now as the most searching are those like Melville and Hawthorne, who did not yield to easy uplift but maintained an acute awareness of the tensions between good and evil, both within man and in the external world. And the new poets—here or abroad—with most conviction of religious truth are those like Auden or Karl Shapiro who are not turning to the Yogi, but are trying to recapture the living truth in such terms as Original Sin and Grace. There is no need to accept Koestler's artificial absolute separation between Change from Without and Change from Within. We can be whole men in a potentially decent society only if we have recourse to both.

Arthur Koestler in Palestine

by Edmund Wilson

The novels of Arthur Koestler have been compared to those of André Malraux and Ignazio Silone. All three of these writers have had first-hand experience of the revolutionary movements of our time, and all three have applied in their fiction, to a greater or less extent, the Communist analysis of society. There is, however, one conspicuous difference between the new novel by Arthur Koestler, *Thieves in the Night* (Macmillan)—I have not read his others— and the books of Malraux and Silone. These latter, though they deal with such political events as the Chinese and Spanish revolutions and the struggle against Fascism in Germany and Italy, are not merely political novels. Here the aims, the ideas, and the actions of specific political efforts are criticized against the background of the general situation of humanity—what Malraux calls *"la condition humaine."* There is, behind the ups and downs of the rebellions and oppressions they chronicle, a conception of the ordinary man which does not allow him to be accounted for completely in terms of Marxist motivations, and an ideal of the extraordinary man which does not present his genius and interests as identical with what is required for the ideal Communist leader. With Malraux, the typical hero is a man in whom the desperate pass to which humanity has been brought in our day has inspired a thirst for power and a need to prove to himself, by exploits in defiance of society, a Nietzschean superiority in intellect and nerve. In the case of Silone's Pietro Spina, the priest, the man of God, comes to life in the political agitator, to console and sustain the people when he discovers that it is impossible to harness them to the shafts of the Communist categories.

Now it is true that one finds also in *Thieves in the Night* some

"Arthur Koestler in Palestine," by Edmund Wilson. From *The New Yorker*, 22 (November 15, 1946), 125-30. Reprinted by permission of Farrar, Strauss & Giroux, Inc.

tendency to displace the attention from the political role of the
protagonist to the kind of personality he is, some interest in a mal-
adjustment which does not exclusively figure as a spur to the rejection of the social group to which he is supposed to belong but
which later continues to operate in connection with the community
of outlaws to which he has attached himself. Yet Koestler does not
make this important, and his neglect of his hero as a character—
to deal at once with the limitations of a fascinating and able book—
results in a novel which, as novel, is rather unsatisfactory. It is not
merely that he allows certain elements to drop into the background
of his picture but that he leaves the picture incomplete. The story
of Joseph himself, as distinguished from the historical drama in
which he becomes involved, has been carelessly put together and is
not really told. This young man is the son of an Englishwoman and
a Russian-Jewish violinist, who, losing his father in childhood, has
never known much about him and has been brought up, playing
cricket and riding, in a large English country house. But his position in the English world has been suddenly and irrevocably snatch-
ed from him. While at Oxford, he had had a love affair with a
woman five years older than himself, who, discovering what Koestler calls "the stigma of the race incised into his flesh," "accused him
of infamy and deception," and "ordered him to...clear out of her
room." She had been influenced by the British blackshirts, and it
must be supposed that Joseph would have realized or found out by
experience that her point of view was rather exceptional; but Koestler makes him from this moment devote himself to a cult of the
memory of his father and associate himself exclusively with his
father's race. Eventually, he has joined the Zionists, and at the
opening of the story, in 1937, we see him as a member of a small
Jewish commune who have come to stake out a claim on an un-
inhabited hill in Palestine. Here he falls deeply in love with a
superior girl from Frankfurt, the daughter of the editor of a liberal
paper, who has been tortured in Germany by the Nazis to make her
betray her father and for whom it has become impossible to marry
or to have a lover because, as a result of this experience, she has
developed a phobia against being touched. When this girl is raped
and murdered by the Arabs, whom the British are now encouraging,
having withdrawn their support from the Jews, the young man,

possessed by a fury for which his work in the commune provides
no outlet, joins an underground organization which is training
Jewish terrorists.

I will not spend more time on this story—of which the first part
seems rather implausible and the second, Joseph's love for Dina,
fails to be moving because it is scarcely real—for the author seems
hardly to take it seriously. It is even perhaps unfair to approach
the book from this direction. Joseph may not be credible as half-
English and brought up in England, and his emotions in connection
with Dina may not be made convincing; but all that is relevant to
Koestler's purpose is to have his hero half a Jew, so that he can
loyally take part in the commune and at the same time criticize the
Jews from a semi-detached point of view, and to equip him with a
personal reason—where one is as good as another—for going over
to the party of violence. The shortcomings of the book as a story of
the adventures of a fictional hero are felt most in the final chapters,
in which Koestler does not find it possible to engineer the kind of
climax that would give us any new revelation of either the meaning
of Joseph's career or the destiny of the Zionist movement. There is
a description of the Zionist riots that occurred when, in May, 1939,
it was announced by the British government that immigration into
Palestine was to stop and that it was no part of British policy "that
Palestine should become a Jewish state"—a description which
might have been written for the newspapers by an exceptionally
gifted reporter; but the narrative is then simply dropped, with
Joseph, one foot in the commune and one in the underground,
assisting at the reception and sendoff of a party of contraband im-
migrants who have come there to found a new settlement. We do
not feel that we have finished a novel; we seem rather to have come
to the end of the latest of a series of dispatches, which leaves the
situation in doubt till new developments can be reported.

But as a series of dispatches, *Thieves in the Night* is satisfying as
few such things are, and almost belongs in the class of *Ten Days that
Shook the World*. To his inquiry into the happenings in Palestine,
Arthur Koestler has brought the trained intelligence of a veteran
of the Left and the excitement of a dramatic imagination. He grati-
fies many curiosities and clears up a good deal of the confusion.
And the types and milieux are so solidly done, the incidents succeed

one another with such naturalness and lively movement that, absorbed by the panorama, you quite forget Joseph's problems. Nor do you have merely the illusion of watching: *Thieves in the Night* is one of those rare feats of journalism which make you feel that you have been there yourself. You invade dirty Arab huts and shrink from the diseased children; you have dinner with the British Commissioner and make conversation with his guests; you walk the streets of Tel Aviv, rather amazed at the new concrete houses and the Europeanized cafés; you are overcome, exploring dark alleys, by the Oriental smells of Jerusalem; and you are baked and benumbed on the barren hills, digging trenches and putting up buildings. Several streams of life go on, entangled and at odds with each other. The Jews, with a home of their own and in contact with the land again, acquire or revive characteristics which they had lost in the ghettos of cities: a new morale, a new physique; the Arabs, upset in their traditional ways by the proximity of modern education and modern agricultural methods, extend their feuding with each other to the Jews—incited by British romantics who passionately admire the Arab and are mimicking Lawrence of Arabia; the British officials in residence, patronizing both parties to the quarrel and holding them at arm's length, play them off against one another as is demanded by British advantage. Finally, we see the Jews, threatened with the abortion of the project into which so much life has been poured, inevitably producing a terrorist wing, a new kind of Jewish belligerence that is driven to resort not merely to ruthlessness and discipline, but to a hate-mongering and mumbo-jumbo that disquietingly recall the Fascists and Nazis.

In its study of social groups and political manifestations, the book is full of the psychological insights which are the only things that make history intelligible and the writing of it a humanistic art. *Thieves in the Night* is not, and it hardly pretends to be, a first-rate contribution to literature, but it is one of the most valuable reports that have been written about the recent events of our bewildered and appalling period.

Palestinian Ice Age

by Isaac Rosenfeld

Arthur Koestler, superior journalist, is also the foremost contemporary problem-novelist. With *Thieves in the Night* he has turned his attention to the Jewish problem and the question of Palestine. Koestler's talent for dramatizing a problem is of a high order; so high, that his dramatic inventions are also, on occasion, happy analytic insights. Thus the dramatization in *Darkness at Noon* of the issues of the Moscow trials outlines what seems to me the only possible explanation of the trials. An advanced knowledge of politics and a sensitivity to its human implications occupy a prominent place in his fiction, as they do in all his work.

The most appealing, but at once the most disconcerting, quality of Koestler's thought is its simplicity. He is master of the epigrammatic flash, the instant generalization which seems to point a conclusion, even if, on afterthought, it is shown to have led nowhere: e.g., his statement, in support of the last war, that we fought against a total lie in the name of a half-truth. He is fond of such polarities as Yogi-Commissar, such dichotomies as "Christ or arithmetic" as alternative principles for the conduct of life, and of phrases such as the one applied to Joseph, the half-Jewish hero of the present novel, whose conversion to the cause of the Jews, after a humiliating experience in an affair with a fascist sympathizer, is expressed in the words, "It had been a curious journey—from Lily's bed to Ezra's Tower in Galilee." It is such simple, pointed reductions that give Koestler the power of speech; where others bog down in the analysis of complexity, he follows his fluent course from problem to problem, secure, apparently, in the thought—assuming it occurs to him— that even if his judgments are only partially correct (and sometimes embarrassingly shallow), a concern with essential problems is of considerable service to the truth.

"Palestinian Ice Age," by Isaac Rosenfeld. From *The New Republic,* 115 (November 4, 1946), p. 592-93.

Koestler's judgments are rarely of the self-questioning kind; he takes too much for granted. Basic to his position are a number of unexamined assumptions, attitudes and moods which are as important, reflexively, to the disclosure of Koestler's habits of mind as they are to his objective opinions. Many of these habits are bad, but they must be counted among his virtues, for it is precisely his limitations, by which he reflects his age, that give his utterances their authenticity for the age.

Thieves in the Night tells the story of the settlement of the Commune of Ezra's Tower in hostile Arab country. The Jewish pioneers move in at night. By sunrise they are at work on fortifications, dugouts, roads, the watchtower and temporary living quarters, and by nightfall have matters well enough in hand to meet and fight off an Arab attack. The Commune endures many hardships but it grows and prospers. The Jews turn into Hebrews as they lose the memories of their persecuted past. The liveliness of their condition, which Koestler calls the extreme condition of mankind, humanity's exposed nerve, shall disappear; their children shall be Hebrew peasants, "unjewish-looking and slightly dull." Meanwhile, the vitality of Jewish life is expressed in its millennial traits: the sharpness, the enthusiasm, the dancing of the *hora,* the "Hebrew prophetic streak [cross-bred] with socialist sectarianism." The story is told for the most part through Joseph's eyes and it is through him that the counterclaims to the growth of a healthy Jewish peasantry are presented: the gifted, sensitive individual member's coming into conflict with the Commune's demands for conformity; the resort to violence and terror against the Arabs and British on the part of the more strong-willed settlers, whose original, exposed Jewish nerve has not been covered up in the new peace. The novel as a whole is one of Koestler's best. It has greater density and drama than *Darkness at Noon* and *Arrival and Departure;* the aspect of being a dramatized problem, which is just about the definition of Koestler's fiction, does not prevent the present novel from achieving a great excitement on its own merits. It reads almost as if a fictional imagination produced it.

But not an extraordinary intelligence. Koestler makes some attempt at a study of Jewish self-hatred in the person of Joseph ("self-hatred is the Jewish form of patriotism") and himself takes advantage of this patriotic privilege to the extent of calling the Jews a race in which the flaws are concentrated, not diluted as in other races. "It's the long inbreeding, I suppose," Joseph remarks to the American correspondent, Dick Matthews:

> They call us the salt of the earth—but if you heap all the salt on one plate it doesn't make a palatable dish. Sometimes I think the Dead Sea is the perfect symbol for us. It is the only big inland lake under sea level, stagnant, with no outlet, much denser than normal water with its concentrated minerals and biting alkaloids; over-salted, over-spiced, saturated. ...

If the Jews are so disliked, it is because there is something dislikable about them. Koestler therefore favors the dilution of Jewishness. In a recent article in *The New York Times Sunday Magazine* Section, after calling for the partition of Palestine into independent Jewish and Arab states, with the admission of as many Jews as possible into the Jewish state, Koestler argued for the assimilation of the rest of the Jews into the Gentile world. In the novel this position is not expressed; here, though he is writing as an imaginative writer, he does not fail to see that the real evidence is all against such a solution. Assimilation was obviously impossible in the worst hour of Jewish history, when one section of the Gentile world was engaged in the extermination of the Jews with the passive support of the rest of the world. And prospects are no better now. Koestler, apparently, does not feel the impact of his own fiction.

It is in the impact it carries as a dramatization of Palestinian politics between 1937 and 1939, with an obvious application to the present, that *Thieves in the Night* achieves its greatest success. At a time when the persecution of the Jews was reaching its peak, and when communal life in Palestine offered the only haven and the only restoration to humanity to the Jews of Europe, the British government issued its White Paper, cutting off all sale of land to Jews, limiting further immigration to 75,000 and condemning millions to death. The *Assimi,* laden with refugees, is intercepted by the coastal patrol within swimming distance of the shore, its passengers are sent back to Hitler. It is against such British crimes that Koestler's indignation rises to its proudest, its best and least compromised expression; and when he describes the action of the extremists, the so-called "Stern Gang," he provides them with a sufficient natural justification. It is as a reporter that he writes his most effective passages on the marching, enraged, leaderless Jews of Jerusalem and Tel-Aviv; but as a reporter with a sense of history, its tragedy and shame.

But once he has done presenting the natural justification of violence and, turning political theoretician, begins to look for a higher justification, all sense and principle desert him. In writing of the underground extremists he repudiates what was the basis of his opposition to Stalinism in *Darkness at Noon* and his other writings: his belief that the end does not justify the means. Koestler emphasizes the fascist character of the underground, whose business, he makes it appear, is to beat the fascists at their own game; and he has even a word of admiration for the way the fascists have been able to combine initiative and imagination with a blind obedience to authority. Now the end does justify the means. It seems to me that the only way Koestler could have justified terrorism would have been to argue that the apparent means of the underground are not true means at all, but forced options: the only choice when no choice is possible. Koestler does argue that no alternative course is open — he ridicules the revolutionaries and the diplomatists alike. When the only way you can act is to imitate the fascists, you imitate the fascists, and there's an end of the matter. And this is not their game, for they had free choice, and we have not. But this is a far cry from his actual resolution of the problem, which is to make a *preferential* selection of terrorist means.

Koestler, moreover, does not set the problem of terrorism in the larger historical context to which it belongs, that of revolutionary action in general. Terrorism seems to have become for him what it was for some non-Marxist or pre-Bolshevist revolutionaries — the whole of strategy, rather than a kind of tactics. He is certain that organized strategy in the socialist sense is now impossible. With the peculiarly masochistic pleasure that many former Marxists now take in yielding to necessity — in their motivation there is present even an element of wickedness: the pleasure one takes in destroying others' illusions — he insists, in effect, that the abandonment of a broad social or international perspective is now forced upon us. The Marxists are involved in a futile chess game, unaware that the rules have been changed. Only sectarian idiots still speak of common action with the Arabs against the British. This is the Ice Age.

Very well, this is the Ice Age. But first of all one must remark that Koestler keeps his pessimism warm by observing how the sectarian idiots shiver, by attributing absurdity in kind to their hopes and by extending the heartiest congratulations to himself on his own absence of illusion. (Koestler as mirror: so many of us are now proud of the fact that we know we have nothing to be proud of.) The Ice Age, furthermore, does strange things to those who survive it. Justice, in Koestler's position, has after all come to be identified with what is; not that what is is just, but that it is all there is of justice. The ideal residuum, the difference between what is and what ought to be, has been traded in for what can be; a bad bargain, for what can be is not enough better than what is (especially to a warm pessimist) to be worth freezing for. The relative concept of a justice which remained relative, partial and unfulfilled so long as the ideal was present has, in the withdrawing of the ideal, become absolute. A clear-cut moral position is therefore no longer held to be possible; on the one hand, Koestler condemns justification of the means by the ends, on the other, he affirms it. This, he insists, is the real measure of our defeat, and he is as helpless as any other man. But soft, sir, you relish this defeat.

Koestler: A Guilty Figure

by V. S. Pritchett

Between imaginative writing and journalism the distinction is easy to make; but in some periods the critic is not required to refine on it. In the nineteenth century the readers of Dickens or Dostoevski could see the journalism of these writers at a glance, and could without difficulty snip an editorial on the Poor Law, or a feature article on the Russian soul and its need to occupy Constantinople, from the imaginative pages. The readers of great European journalists like Herzen, Engels, and, in our own time, Trotsky, were in no danger of mistaking these writers for artists in an important sense, for artists towered above them. Today the relation has changed.

It is generally agreed that the last decade has been unpropitious for the imaginative writer and that the distinguished work of our years has been fragmentary and small in compass; and as the imaginative writer has receded, so the journalist has advanced. It is he, the obstreperous, overgrown child of events, who has towered and glowered; and it becomes necessary once more to mark his difference from the creative writer. The task is delicate because the distinction may be thought invidious. It is not, for many imaginative writers have been journalists in the past decade and with every advantage to the range of their interests and their talent. The digestive process of journalism is coarser than that of art, and we have lived through a period when a coarse digestion became indispensable. The journalist has had the task of accommodating violence to the private stomach and of domesticating the religious, revolutionary, and national wars in the private conscience. He has been the intermediary between our private and public selves and, in doing this office, has become a hybrid and representative figure, the vacillating and tortured Hamlet expressing our common disinclinations and our private guilt.

"Koestler: A Guilty Figure," by V. S. Pritchett. From *Harper's Magazine*, 196 (January 1948), 84-92.

For it is typical of the contemporary journalist that his case history goes with him. Like Hamlet, he travels with his court of private disasters, his ghosts, his Ophelias, even his Rosencrantz and Guildenstern and though we may often think the sight ridiculous, we must give him the credit for attempting the creation of a new kind of first person singular, a new hero, who can "take" the assaults of decivilization, who has invented a certain style or personal carriage which enables him to face the spectacle of mass suffering and official medievalism, with passion, stoicism, and humanity. To him his style, his air, is as important as his humanity; and, eventually, we may be sure that artists will collect his vestiges, as once they eagerly collected the sacred relics of Byronism.

To the journalism and the reporting of the higher kind the work of Arthur Koestler is a copious guide. He is not at the level of Malraux or Silone, for he lacks the hard self-control of the Frenchman, the fierce brain and luminous sensibility of the Italian. Koestler's gift is bold and fresh, but it is theatrical. He is the declaiming and compelling actor. No one has known better than he when to drop what he is doing and rush to document the latest convulsion. In this fashion, he has run through the political infections of our generation—through Marxism, Leninism, anti-Stalinism—and practice has accompanied theory. He has known and documented the political prisons and torture houses. He has neighbored the class described in his book, *Scum of the Earth,* the human wreckage of the Left which Fascism scattered over Europe. How much in his writing is personal experience and how much is an intense imaginative identification with the people he describes is not important; or rather, only the identification is important. It is passionate because it is moral; it is complex because it is at once theatrical and aware of itself.

There are other qualities: Koestler is more than a simple reporter. He is intellectually volatile; it is second nature for him to generalize about events; he is politically trained, and likes to be politically bespattered. It is the business of the journalist to interview everything and Koestler is able to interview philosophy, science, economics, history, and to come back with a notebook full of general ideas which are put to dramatic use. For the rest, the traits of the profession are emphasized in him by his lack of roots. He was born a displaced person: half-Hungarian, half-Jew, he was educated in Vienna, worked in Germany and Palestine, lived in France. He has been created to wander without mundane allegiances. His allegiances were always to the world of ideas or myth; and when these failed, to the world of random physical events. Guilt and self-pity have been the price. With some exceptions—Strindberg is one—imaginative writers appear to allay their neuroses in works of art; but the neuroses of the journalist are exacerbated by his special opportunities for seeing life.

Yet definitions like these do not bring Koestler into the intimate scope of the English critic. He is separated from us by the education and the politics of the Continent, by the vast difference between the large, stable middle-class in England and the small, precarious middle-class of Central Europe. He can easily dazzle us because we have no cafe' conversation and no cafe' writers. We have no skill in playing poker with ideas. We are not trained to pretend that things which are entirely different may (for the pleasure of effect) be assumed to be opposites. We have no eternal students. We have no intelligentsia. These singularities have led Koestler himself to as complete and conventional misreading of English life as any that have been done by Continental writers. (See *The Yogi and the Commissar.*) We must assume that our judgment of him will suffer from similar difficulties of contact.

We come nearest to him in *Scum of the Earth*. This is partly because the book is a personal record of the events at the fall of France where, at last, English experience came close to the experience of the Continent. A second reason is that here Koestler has cleaned his slate and is putting down just what he saw and heard and, with emotion, is pulling down the curtain on a period. This report is alive; it is packed with human beings; it is resilient and almost buoyant. He is in his natural element, or rather in one of his natural elements: anarchy and disillusion. His eyes are skinned for every incident as, somber and sardonic—but not with detachment—he notes down the fates of his friends. This book (and *The Gladiators*) contains his least opaque writing.

But we first heard of Koestler in *The Spanish Testament* and here a play is beginning, not coming to an end. We see the sullen sky over Vigo harbor glowing "under an evil spell." It is the Koestler spell. We are in for melodrama. "The constriction in the throat that affects a whole town, a whole population, like an epidemic": as in the theater, generalizations, simplifications. The characters wear the makeup of revolution. This writer does not appear to know Spanish history, but he knows current Marxism. He is briefed. He is in control, and can switch on and off when effects are needed. Sardonic anger, raw humor, and the punctures of anthropological inquiry let the wind out of his hysterical passages at the right moment. All this is good journalism, but compared, say, with Borkenau on Spain, it is slapdash. Koestler was a smatterer, and the only thing of value that emerged was personal: *Dialogue with Death.* There have been finer, more sensitive, more humane, and more objective accounts of life in Spanish prisons than Koestler's, for Koestler had to be the leading actor, and he writes with one wall of the prison down; but the attempt at a personal revelation is intellectually impressive, and precisely in the study of hysteria which elsewhere in his writing is his least attractive quality. In the end, when the curtain goes down in *Spanish Testament* we are not entirely convinced or convicted. Perhaps because we have been overconvinced. The impression remains after other books by Koestler. Against ourselves must be put his strongest card: he has had to combat the English unwillingness to face the appalling facts of medieval atrocity on the Continent.

II

Yet this may not be the explanation of our uneasiness. The source may be literary: Koestler has a voice, an urgent voice, vital, voluble, and lively, above all never boring—a voice, but an arid and mechanical style. On the face of it this is an unkind criticism to make of a displaced writer who is not writing in his own tongue, who has to make shift to write our own and has mastered it. But we suspect that no language is an inconvenience to him; language is a machine; not even in his own language, we feel, has he any love of words or any sense of their precision and grace. Here is a passage from *The Yogi and the Commissar,* and I think the manner itself forbids belief in the argument, and leaves us with the sensation that Koestler himself would only half-believe in it if he could express it simply, for it is only half-true:

The law of the novel-perspective prescribes that it is not enough for the author to create "real life," he must also locate its geometrical place in a co-ordinate system, the axes of which are represented by the dominating facts, ideas, and tendencies of his time; he must fix its position in an n-dimensional space-time continuum. The real Sylvia spins around the center of a narrow family-vortex of conditioning factors, whereas the author, in promoting her to novel life, places her in the center of a vortex formed by the great trade winds, typhoons, depressions, and hurricanes of her time. Of course he need not describe or even mention them. But implicitly they must be there.

Koestler uses words as thought-saving gadgets from the ironmongery counter, and draws especially on the vocabulary of science and economics which is paralyzed by patents. Like the Latin tag, they may appeal to the vanity; and the Central European mind appears to be susceptible to technical coagulations, but neither exactitude nor pleasure issues from them. The love of jargon suggests the lack of an instinct or a sense, and suggests a deaf and arbitrary nature.

The deficiency is more damaging to Koestler's reporting than to his earliest novels. Shaky as some passages in *The Gladiators* are— it was his first "English" novel, and, presumably, a translation— they are pretty free of vices of style. The jargon of Marx, Freud, Einstein, would have been grotesque in a story of ancient Rome and the Spartacus revolt. We are captured at once in this novel by the sardonic vivacity of the author, the raciness of his reporting, his light mastery of the novelist's and historian's material, even by his boyish humor. We also feel a quality which is rare in the melodramas that come after: the sense of the human tragedy and a pity that is truly pitched and moving. That feeling for tragedy is never recovered, and in my opinion *The Gladiators* is his most impressive book. No personal hatred, no extraneous obsession with persecution or guilt, clutters the running of the narrative, or impedes the growth of the argument: for though the matter of the Trotsky-Stalin conflict is present in the chapter on "the law of detours" and is implicit in the main crisis of the book, Koestler has not yet projected himself into the Moscow trials. Success destroys: the revolutions that fail preserve their myth, and to Koestler faith and myth are everything. Another reason for Koestler's excellence in this book is that it has a settled subject, set in the remote past, and history has agreed on it. By gift a reporter, he is a hundred times better in recording what is given than in contriving imaginatively what is not; with him, controversy simply brings out the "old soldier" of the clinics.

The subject of *The Gladiators* is the rising of the slaves under Spartacus, their race to triumph, the tragic split with Crixus, and the final defeat. On the one hand the laxity and shamelessness, the experience and corruption of Rome are comically and diversely rendered with a ribaldry and a talker's scholarship that recall the early Aldous Huxley. These Roman portraits are plump and impudent medallions, cheerfully unclassical; they are the footnotes of Gibbon turned into agreeable and scabrous cartoons. On the other hand is the raw, rushing, high-voiced rebellion, tearing down the roads, laughing, shouting, guzzling, raping, killing. The wings of the traditional humane ideal raise riot above its own lusts; the brotherhood of the camp makes the spirit flesh. There is a pity for the mindless hopes and follies of simple people: this is the only book of Koestler's to show us the lowly material of revolution, the simple man who, even in his excess, does not wish to die, and whose last look, as he falls, is of surprise. (In the later books, the dying of the revolutionary leaders has lost all human quality; it has become a transaction of policy.) The masses in *The Gladiators* are incapable of salvation, and between the Gadarene downrush which Crixus will lead, and the slow, painful political course for which the mind of Spartacus is pathetically groping, they choose the former. Spartacus, who cannot stand the screams of his own prisoners, is overwhelmed by the necessity of being a tyrant. He parts company with half his horde; "objectively" he ought to have killed them.

We feel the earth under our feet in this book, and whether or not it has the developed qualities of a novel is not important. In fact, it is a collection of brilliantly placed episodes, linked by a commentary; and growing characters are not required. (This is fortunate, because it turns out in his later work that Koestler has little power to create or sustain large characters.) All that is required in this book is that his pictures of people shall have instantaneous physical reality— Spartacus himself needs very little to fix him in our mind's eye— and that the atmosphere and the feeling shall be actual, like the news. The best of Koestler is in a passage like the following on the fate of the Praetor; and the end of the passage indicates where Koestler goes wrong:

On foot—for his horse had been left with the robbers—the bald-headed Praetor Clodius Glaber climbed down into the plain. He had been separated from his fleeing soldiers, and walked through the night, alone. He strayed from the trodden path, stumbled over the crooked, stony edge of a vineyard, looked around. The vineyard, studded with pointed stakes, looked like a graveyard by the stars' light. It was very quiet; bandits and Vesuvius dimmed to unreality, Rome and Senate were blotted out; yet one more deed asked to be done. He opened his cloak, felt the place with his fingers, gently pressed the sword-point to it.

The deed asked to be done, but it was only now he understood its full meaning. Little by little the point must be driven home; little by little it must tear through tissue, cut tendons and muscles, splinter the ribs. Not till then the lung is reached, tender, mucous, thinly veined; it must be ripped asunder. Now a slimy shell, and now the heart itself, a bulbous bag of blood—its touch beyond imagination. Had ever a man accomplished this? Well he might, with a sudden thrust, perhaps. But once you knew of the process and every one of its stages, you would never be able to do it.

"Death," up to now a word like any other, seemed removed into unattainable distance. All the relatives of Death, such as Honor, Shame, and Duty, exist for him only who has no ken of reality. For reality, mucous, unspeakably delicate, with its mesh of thin veins, is not made to be torn to bits by some pointed object. And now Praetor Clodius Glaber knows that dying is unutterably stupid—more stupid still than life itself.

He realizes that his shoes are full of pebbles. He sits down on a stone and empties the shoes; he observes that the pebbly discomfort had been a responsible element of his despair. As compared to the ignominious defeat of his army, the sharp little pebbles—seven in all —admittedly shrink into ridiculous insignificance. But how can you sift the important from the unimportant if both speak to your senses with equal vehemence? His tongue and palate are still covered with the stale taste of interrupted sleep; a few forgotten grapes lurk between the vines. He plucks a few, looks around; only the stars are witnessing the curious sequence of his actions, and their sight is no rebuke to him.

He feels ashamed and yet he must admit that his actions are in no way senseless; no amount of philosophy can alter the fact that grapes were made to be eaten. Besides, he has never before enjoyed grapes as much. He sips their juice together with the tears of an unexplained emotion. He smacks his lips with defiance and shame.

And night with the lights of its indifferent stars gave as a further knowledge into Praetor Clodius Glaber: all pleasure, not only defined versions of it, and Life itself, are based on age-old, secret shamelessness.

Why can't these Central Europeans learn when to stop? The myth of "age-old, secret shamelessness"! Not *another* myth, we exclaim, not a new thesis, a new antithesis, a new synthesis!

The real core of Koestler's thought in *The Gladiators* — it is taken up again in a moving passage toward the end of his latest book *Thieves in the Night* — is in the words of the Essene to Spartacus:

"Prophecies are never worth anything," said the Essene. "I explained that before, but in the meantime you've been asleep. Prophecies do not count, he who receives them counts."

Spartacus lay in thought, his eyes open.

"He who receives them will see evil days," he said after a while.

"Aye," said the Essene. "He'll have a pretty rotten time."

"He who receives them," said Spartacus, "will have to run and run, on and on, until he foams at the mouth and until he has destroyed everything in his way with his great wrath. He'll run and run, and the Sign won't let go of him, and the demon of wrath will tear through his entrails."

Spartacus listens to the Essene through the night, until the sky lightens: "The black shadows in his eye sockets had, as it were, evaporated. ... Spartacus looked again at the glowing East and at the mountain whose everyday shape gradually broke the spell of its nightly distortion."

Night, dawn, noon, the spell: the symbols are theatrical.

III

Spartacus fails, but now the dawn has come; we are moving towards the success at Noon, the darkness at Noon which is the corruption of success. This is an ancient and haunting Jewish theme. The race, by numberless pronouncements of Jehovah, has been fated to be destroyed in success, to be searching forever.

Darkness at Noon is a *tour de force,* a book terrifying and claustrophobic, an intellectual thriller. The efficiency, the speed, the smooth order of the narrative as it runs fast to its end, are extraordinary. Here is the story of a man arguing his way (or being argued) toward the confession of crimes he has not committed, an interpretation of the Moscow trials, a dramatized examination of the problem of ends and means. As a novelist, Koestler has a superb gift for the handling of argument in a living way; he knows when to break off, when to slip into the personal or the small incident, when to digress into the minor character, where to tighten the screw. Rubashov, the accused, makes the pace all through the story; he is an alert, intelligent man—a brain, where Spartacus was passive. And occasionally, like a sudden fragment of sunlight in this gray and horrifying book, horrifying in its grim pistol-barrel logic, moments of human illumination occur in Rubashov. They are moving. But when all praise is given, *Darkness at Noon* remains a melodrama. Rubashov and Gletkin are a sad pair of Jesuits consumed and dulled as human beings by their casuistry. The Communists have taken over the doctrine of original sin from the Roman Catholic Church, and have tacked the Calvinist doctrine of Predestination on to it; but they have dispelled the visionary and emotional quality of these dogmas, with the dull acrimony of the makers of company bylaws. An irredeemable dreariness surrounds the lives of Rubashov and Gletkin. They are not "great"; they are merely committee men or chess players.

The book is not tragedy. Yet to be destroyed by your own church or by your own beliefs ought to be tragic. It is surely tragic for the young to destroy the old. There were (if Koestler had not been so gifted in the art of making a case) tragic springs in Rubashov's history. Somewhere in the tale, Ivanov (one of the Inquisitors who is drugging himself with drink) remarks that the murders of Raskolnikov were trivial because they served, or failed to serve, private ends; had they served the ends of the collective morality, they would have been significant. But in *Darkness at Noon* the official killing of Rubashov to serve the collective end fails to reach this high standard. It is a police act, not a tragedy, the end of a case. Koestler could reply that the casuistry of Gletkin & Co. has destroyed the concept of tragedy on the collective plane; but the casuistry is Koestler's. Rubashov, who has betrayed so many people in the name of "objectivity," has destroyed himself in advance, and is simply getting what is coming to him. By inference, the same will happen to

Gletkin. The two rascals are agreed. Wolf, as the Czarist officer says, eats wolf. Great ideas are in conflict, but in this book they are not embodied in great men.

We have to turn to the greatest of all novels about the revolutionary, Dostoevski's *The Possessed,* to see that *Darkness at Noon* is a powerful book, but not an imaginative work of the highest kind. It has the intensity of obsession, the interest of surgery, but no largeness. It is a document, pulled up by the roots from a native soil. The revolutionaries of *The Possessed* are living people with biographies, and they are set among other living people. Russia breathes in Dostoevski's novel, its landscape, its towns, its climate, its history, and grants them the pardon of time and place. For it is evident, from our postwar contacts with them, that the Russians are as Dostoevski drew them: a people living by wont in a natural atmosphere of suspicion and mistrust, and consumed by fantasies. *The Possessed* is soaked in its own people, grows out of Russian soil. It is felt.

Compared with *The Possessed, Darkness at Noon* grows out of nowhere. It is allegory. Yet even the Party is not the same in all countries, and the problem of ends and means is decided not by moralists, but by temperament, feeling, tradition. The objection to *Darkness at Noon* is not that it has overstated its case, but that it has stated only a case; the book understates its field of human, psychological, and historical reference. Koestler's own mind is like a prison, with its logical corridors, its dazzling but monotonous lighting, the ingenious disposition of its control towers, its traverses and walls. And there are also the judas slots through which we are led to observe the sudden, shocking, physical revelation; those cells from which the bangings of hysteria break out and those silent cells where the dingy human being stands in his day dream; and, outside, the courtyard where the man circles, dragging his shame in his scraping feet. No normal emotion, above all no love, can be felt there, but only the self-love and self-hatred of the prisoner. And Koestler, who occupies this prison, is like some new and enterprising prison governor, humane enough, but more and more attached to the place and infected with the growing belief that the guilty are ourselves, the free, the people outside. This is a position he shares with the Communist intellectuals of his generation. Their habit of hypnotizing and magnetizing a subject by the incantations of repetitive argument, so that it becomes rigid, is his. *Darkness at Noon* might be called a major act of literary hypnosis. And the argument is so successful and complete that we begin ceasing to believe in its human application the moment we put the book down.

IV

After *Darkness at Noon* there is a decline. The tight organization of Koestler's gifts goes slack. Disillusion brought his power to a climax, and since then he has descended to nihilism. *Arrival and Departure* is an attack upon belief itself, due to an unfortunate encounter with psychoanalysis: "If one wanted to explain why Peter had behaved as he did, one had to discard from the beginning his so-called convictions and ethical beliefs. They were mere pretexts of the mind, phantoms of a more intimate reality. It did not matter whether he was a hero of the Proletariat or a martyr of the Catholic Church; the real clue was this suspect craving for martyrdom." More accurately, this book is Koestler's attack upon himself as a member of the small middle-class intelligentsia of the Continent, and it ends by justifying isolation. The Cause has been thrown over and humanity goes with it. Koestler appears to have had a theatrical view of faith; it was a vision, not a bond. By a really crass misreading of Freud the neuroses of the revolutionaries are made to cancel the traditions of humanitarianism, indeed any strivings of the mind. The civilized, the believing and creating mind is dismissed. Peter solves his conflicts by refusing to recognize one side of them, and after he had exploded his beliefs goes off to fight nevertheless because "reasons do not matter."

Intellectually a rotten book, it has all the old skill in story-telling, the old lack of acceptable characters; an incapacity to describe love — love equals lust, etc. — but a terrifying power to describe torture. The effect is overpowering. One could do with the old framework of good and evil to hold this picture in, and the framework existed if Koestler had cared to recognize it. The despised liberal English and Americans of the ordinary kind were impelled to fight and destroy the nation which committed these atrocities. Koestler's atrocities appear to have been taken out of the moral scheme and to have become pornographic. He is like Ivanov in *Darkness at Noon,* who said that ever since the invention of the steam engine, there has been no normality, only war. A remark that is deeply untrue. There is always normality. *Arrival and Departure* shows those vices of style —the use of jargon—which have marked his essays, and the psychoanalysis is too *voulu* for words.

With his last book, *Thieves in the Night,* Koestler returns to something nearer the mood of *The Gladiators,* and his ambivalent attitude to violence—and to ends and means—is almost decided. He has come full circle, i.e. he is *very nearly* prepared to justify violence; or rather he has quite decided to throw out justification. He is among the people whom he really envies and admires, the violent people, the people with grenades in their lorries. This is an old legacy from Communism; one can see it in Malraux also. If anything, Koestler is more depressed by the Zionists' capacity as colonists than by their readiness for killing; practical capacity has no Byronism. We have the suspicion that the Neanderthalers of *Darkness at Noon* are being reproduced in the Promised Land. Can it be that the inhabitants of Utopias are always dull and muttonish?

> I have watched them ever since they arrived—these stumpy, dumpy girls with their rather coarse features, big buttocks, and heavy breasts, physically precocious, mentally retarded, overripe and immature at the same time; and these raw arse-slapping youngsters, callow, dumb, and heavy, with their aggressive laughter and unmodulated voices, without traditions, manners, form, style. ...
>
> Their parents were the most cosmopolitan race of the earth—they are provincial and chauvinistic. Their parents were sensitive bundles of nerves with awkward bodies—*their* nerves are whipcords and their bodies those of a horde of Hebrew Tarzans roaming in the hills of Galilee. Their parents were intense, intent, overstrung, overspiced—they are tasteless, spiceless, unleavened, and tough. Their parents were notoriously polyglot—they have been brought up in one language which had been hibernating for twenty centuries before being brought artificially back to life. ...

But the Joseph of *Thieves in the Night* has found what Peter of *Arrival and Departure* had defined as a psychological aberration: a Cause. More than a Cause: something that none of the Koestler characters has ever had—the lack is their fatal weakness in debate, a nutritional deficiency of Marxist teaching—a country. It is the embryo country, the almost theoretical country of Zionism, but, still, a country. In his youth, Koestler had lived for a time in the Jewish communities of Palestine, but had, for some reason, tired of them and left; now, once violence has arisen, his personal interest and his alert journalist eye for the topical story has been stirred. The truth is, of course, that he is cosmopolitan and European; that is his real virtue politically; he sees the interaction and unity of European events, and this rational attitude is clearly in conflict with his new Faith, and so much so that scepticism, detachment, the yearning not to be committed is the impression that still survives the rifle shots and the Hallelujahs. Such a conflict makes an excellent basis for Koestler's best vein—his talk—and this book has some readable passages.

> Joseph looked around the terrace and sighed. The khamsin lay on people's faces like a spasm. The women were plump, heavy-chested, badly and expensively dressed. The men sat with sloping shoulders and hollow chests, thinking of their ulcers. Each couple looked as if they were carrying on a quarrel under cover of the *Merry Widow.*
> "I can't blame the Gentiles if they dislike us," he said.
> "That proves you are a patriot," said Matthews. "Since the days of your prophets, self-hatred has been the Jewish form of patriotism."
> Joseph wiped his face. The khamsin was telling on him. He felt sick of it all: Judaism, Hebraism, the whole cramped effort to make something revive which had been dead for two thousand years.
> "It is all very well for you to talk as a benevolent outsider," he said. "The fact is, we are a sick race. Tradition, form, style, have all gone overboard. We are a people with a history but no background.... Look around you, and you'll see the heritage of the ghetto. It is there in the wheedling lilt of the women's voices, and in the way the men hold themselves, with that frozen shrug about their shoulders."
> "I guess that shrug was their only defence. Otherwise the whole race would have gone crackers."

The possibility that the terrorists are really Fascist or copying Fascist methods raises the old bugbear about ends and means, and these discussions are boring.

The central figure, narrator and diarist of this report is now, for the first time, English, an English half-Jew. A naïve snobbery is dis ̈ closed here; he belongs to that romantic idol of the Continent, the English country gentry. It is the Disraeli touch. The consequence is that when this character goes to Palestine, he has a low social opinion of the British ruling class who do not come out of the top drawer. One lady—imagine it—has an official position and yet is only the daughter of a sergeant. The only real "lady" is an agreeable sketch, but women have always to be punished in Koestler's novels, and she is made to go through a boring official dinner when afflicted by her periods. Koestler's attitude to sex has always been neurotic—least in *The Gladiator*—and, in one of his articles, he threatens to raise the question of the menarche, no doubt as a new myth in the space-time continuum.

Bedeviled by his journalistic habit of treating differences as opposites—it makes a brighter page—Koestler can only draw the Jewish colonists with ironical sympathy and vigor, by covering the Arabs and the English with riducule.

As we ourselves—see *Passage to India,* George Orwell, etc.— have a robust tradition of satire at the expense of our own people, Koestler's looks thin and conventional; the attack on the Arabs, since it is rarely done in English, is fresher, but historically silly. All the same, the bias of the book works to its advantage as a piece of reporting, but only in the first half, that is, say, up to the rape of the girl Dina. The narrative is brisk and dramatic, the picture of the colony is in full color, the description of its way of living tolerant and moving. We see an Old Testament world; but argued, of course, and enlivened by Koestler's short, snorting, schoolboy humor. After the rape—and rape or lust without love is a special interest of Koestler's: down to fundamentals, strip the pretences, debunk, be honest, away with liberal and *petit bourgeois* prevarications in the bedroom—after the rape, suspiciously enough, the novel disintegrates and wanders around, and Koestler's doubts appear. The story ends in 1939, which is very lucky for the Anglo-Jewish hero who, in any case, is going to be violent, not with bombs after all, but with a wireless station.

One new quality appears in *Thieves in the Night;* an interest in landscape. The descriptions of Galilee are imaginative. Koestler's talent has always been for the hard, surprising, physical image that stamps a person, a crowd, a place on the mind; and now he is extending this poetic interest to places. It brings an amenity up to now uncommon in his work. We welcome it, for in his intense and strung-up work there have been no points of rest; the vice of the "dynamic" conception of life is that it does not record the consolations of inertia, and never contemplates a beautiful thing. His attempts consciously to inject beauty have ended in the sentimental.

Thieves in the Night is an improvement on *Arrival and Departure* but it represents the coarsening and mechanization of a talent. One looks back upon his novels. What is the final impression? They are not novels: they are reports, documentaries, briefs, clinical statements, animated cartoons of a pilgrim's regress from revolution. They are material, formative material: their opponents, as well as their disciples, are formed by them. The effect is hypnotic. It is a paradox that these lively and fast-moving books are, at a second glance, not moving at all. Koestler has fixed them, made them static; it is he with his "case" who is on the move; the story and the people do not move of themselves at all. Our eye is following him and not them.

The result is that, underlying the superficial excitement, a bored sensation of unbelief is built up—why read about people who merely illustrate an argument and are foils for the author? Quickly the people recede before the inevitable half-truths of a magnetizing talker with a good conceit of himself; and while he rarely makes a dull remark, he also rarely makes one that common experience does not flatly contradict.

And yet the confidence with which Koestler grasps important themes makes the continued privacy of the English novel look eccentric. It commonly has been eccentric, but at any rate we have no novelist of the social or public conscience who has Koestler's scope or force—no journalist or reporter either. It is the price we pay for our lack of interest in general ideas for their own sake; empiricism is not dramatic. General ideas become, however, an infatuation; for example, it may be that the Soviet runs a police State, forced labor camps, etc., because Russia has always had these things, and not because of a specific ethical lapse. It may be that Koestler has imposed a Central European efficiency upon the Russian scene in *Darkness at Noon.* Perhaps the English novelist is wise to avoid general ideas and to stick to life as it is presented to himself, and to leave what he doesn't know to the newspapers and the Blue Books. For the novels of Koestler are skeletal. They are like the steel frameworks of modern buildings before the bricks go in; and up there shaking all over with the vibration of the thing, is Koestler furiously concentrating on his pneumatic riveter. A guilty figure: he can't quite get over an old wish that it was a machine-gun, and the principle is maddeningly similar. So guilty does he feel that presently he stops work, harangues the crowd below, and the building is never completed. It remains, a stimulus, an incitement to others, an imposing outline against the sky.

Koestler's Dilemmas

by Maurice Merleau-Ponty

"That is what they want to set up in France," exclaimed an anti-Communist after reading *Darkness at Noon*.[1] "How exciting it must be to live under this regime!" exclaimed a sympathizer of Russian origin who had emigrated in 1905. The first character has forgotten that all regimes are criminal, that Western liberalism rests upon the forced labor of the colonies and twenty wars, that from an ethical standpoint the death of a Negro lynched in Louisiana, or of a native in Indonesia, Algeria, or Indochina is no less excusable than Rubashov's death; he forgets that communism does not invent violence but finds it already institutionalized, that for the moment the question is not to know whether one accepts or rejects violence, but whether the violence with which one is allied is "progressive" and tends toward its own suspension or toward self-perpetuation; and, finally, that in order to decide this question the crime has to be set in the logic of a situation, in the dynamics of a regime and into the historical totality to which it belongs, instead of judging it by itself according to that morality mistakenly called "pure" morality.

The second character has forgotten that violence — anguish, pain, and death — is only appealing in imagination, in art and written history. The most peaceloving men are able to speak of Richelieu and Napoleon without a shudder. One should try to imagine how Urbain Grandier saw Richelieu and how the Duc d'Enghien viewed Napoleon. The remoteness and inertia of past events transforms a crime into an historical necessity and casts a pale shadow over the

"Koestler's Dilemmas," by Maurice Merleau-Ponty. From *Humanisme et Terreur; Essai sur le Probleme Communiste* © 1947, Editions Gallimard; English translation copyright © 1969 by Beacon Press. Reprinted by permission of Beacon Press.

[1]Arthur Koestler, *Darkness at Noon,* Translated by Daphne Hardy, London, Jonathan Cape, 1940. [All quotations are from this English translation rather than the French edition used by Merleau-Ponty — Translator of English edition.].

victim. But which one of Richelieu's academic admirers would kill Urbain Grandier with his own hands? What administrator would himself kill the natives whose deaths he brings about in building a colonial railroad? But the past and what is distant have been and are still lived by men who had and still have only one life to live and the screams of a single man condemned to death are unforgettable.

The anti-Communist refuses to see that violence is universal while the exalted sympathizer refuses to see that no one can look violence in the face. Neither one of them could have read *Darkness at Noon* carefully if he opposes these two facts. Even if it does not pose the question properly, the book raises the problem of our times. That is enough for it to have aroused a lively interest. It is also enough for it to have been not properly *read*, because the questions which haunt us are precisely those which we refuse to formulate. Let us then try to understand this famous but poorly understood book.

Rubashov always dealt with external things and historical processes. It would have been difficult for him to have had to determine his own conduct: the fate of other men as well as his personal destiny unfolded before him, in the world of things, in the making of the Revolution, its success and its spread. What was he beyond a certain X upon whom were imposed tasks clearly called for by the situation? Not even the danger of death could bring him to withdraw into himself: to a revolutionary a man's death is not the end of a world but an agency which cancels itself out. Death is only a particular instance or an extreme limit of historical inactivity and that is why revolutionaries do not say that an adversary has died but that he has been "suppressed physically." For Rubashov and his comrades the "I" was both so unreal and so indecent that they ridiculed it by referring to it as the "grammatical fiction." Humanity, values, virtues, the mutual reconciliation of men, were not in their opinion ends to be reached by reason but possibilities of the proletariat which it was a matter of bringing to power.

For years then Rubashov had lived in ignorance of the subjective. It matters little that Richard is a long-standing and devoted militant, if he weakens, if he disputes the official line, he will be expelled. It is not a question of knowing whether or not the dockers want to unload the oil sent by the homeland of the Revolution to a reactionary government: by prolonging the boycott, the country of the Revolution would risk losing a market. Their industrial development counts for more than the consciousness of the masses. The leaders of the dockers' cell will be expelled. For his own part Rubashov treats himself no better than the others. He believes that the Party leadership is mistaken and he says so. Once arrested, he disavows his oppositionist standpoint, not to save his life, but to save his political life and to stick within history where he has always been. One may wonder how he could love Arlova. Indeed, it is a strange love. Once only she tells him, "You can always do with me whatever you want." And never anything more. Not a word from her when she is broken by the Party cell. Not a word from her the evening she visits Rubashov. And not a word from Rubashov in her defense. He only speaks of her to denounce her when asked by the Party. Honor, dishonor, sincerity, falsehood—such words have no meaning for the man of history. There is only *objective* treason and *objective* merit. The traitor is he who *in fact* deserts the country of the Revolution as it stands, its leadership and its institutions. All the rest is psychology.

When despised, psychology avenges itself; the individual and the state, once confounded in the early stages of the Revolution, later reappear in confrontation. The masses are no longer the vehicle of the state, they are its subjects. Decisions are no longer submitted to discussion throughout the Party, they are imposed through discipline. Unlike in the beginning of the Revolution, policy is no longer based upon a continuous analysis of the world revolutionary movement, nor is it seen any more as the direct extrapolation of the spontaneous course of history. The theoreticians run after the decisions reached on the basis of power in order to rationalize them despite the indifference of power. Bit by bit Rubashov becomes acquainted with that subjectivity which stands back from events and evaluates them. Arrested once more, and this time cut off from action and historical events, it is not just the voices of the masses and the rejected militants that he believes he hears: even his class enemy takes on a human shape for him once more. The reactionary officer who occupies the cell next to his—a woman's man, infatuated with honor and personal courage—is no longer just one of the White Guards whom Rubashov had shot during the Revolution, but *some-*

one to whom one can talk by tapping on the wall in the language of
prisoners everywhere in the world. For the first time Rubashov sees
the Revolution from the standpoint of the White Guard and he
realizes that no one can feel justified in the eyes of those on whom
he has inflicted violence. He "understands" the White Guards'
hate, he "forgives," but, from then on, even his revolutionary past
is in question. And yet it was precisely in order to liberate men that
he had used violence against some men. He does not think he was
wrong. But he is no longer innocent. There remain all those con-
siderations which it was necessary to neglect. There remains another
claim than that of history and the revolutionary enterprise, another
criterion than that of reason absorbed in the calculation of efficacy.
There remains the need to undergo what one has made others submit to in order to re-establish with them a reciprocity and communication to which revolutionary action does not accommodate
itself. Rubashov is to die in opposition, and in silence, like all those
whom he executed in his own day.

All the same, if it is men who matter, why should he be more
faithful to the dead than to the living? Outside of prison, there are
all those who, for better or worse, are following the path on which
Rubashov set them. If he dies in silence, he abandons these men
with whom he has fought and his death will not enlighten them.
Moreover, what other path is there to show them? Perhaps what is
happening is that more and more and bit by bit we have arrived at
a new politics. To break with the regime would mean disowning the
revolutionary past to which he owes his origins. Yet every time he
thinks of 1917 it is clear to Rubashov that the Revolution was necessary and that in the same circumstances he would be part of it, even
knowing where it leads. If one takes on the past, one must also take
on the present. To die in silence Rubashov would have had first
to change his morality—he would have had to prefer the vertigo of
"testimony," to prefer the immediate and crazy affirmation of values
to action in the world and upon history. Testimony before whom?
All during his youth he had learned that to resort to this super-
terrestrial pleading was the most subtle of mystifications, since
it authorizes us to forsake men as they are and makes us abandon an
effective morality for an ethereal ethics. He had learned that true
morality laughs at morality, that the only way of remaining true to

values is to turn outward in order to attain, as Hegel says, "the reality of the moral idea," and that the short cut of spontaneous feeling is the way of immorality. It was in the name of historical exigencies that he formerly defended dictatorship and the violence it inflicted upon beautiful souls.[2] What could he say today in reply to anyone relating his speeches to him? Would it be that formerly dictatorship based its decisions upon a theoretical analysis and a free discussion of viewpoints? That is true. But, once the line was chosen, it was necessary to obey, and for those who do not see clearly, the dictatorship of truth is no different from sheer force. Once one has defended the former, one has to accept the latter. And what if the very hardening of the dictatorship and the renunciation of theory were imposed by the world situation? Rubashov would give in.

As soon as he returns to the hard Marxist rule which demands that a man be described not by his intentions but by what he does, and that action be evaluated not according to its subjective meaning but its objective sense, then again the pattern of Rubashov's life is transformed. First of all, because some thoughts and words, which taken singly remain in the indeterminacy of the subjective, now reinforce one another and form a coherent system. The testimony on the stand is very far from being false. Rubashov even remarks on the meticulous reporting of certain events and conversations. If there is any falsehood it lies in this very preciseness and in fixing once and for all on paper a phrase or an idea born of the moment. But is even that a distortion? It is not unjust to impute to Rubashov certain sarcastic remarks and amusing comments but also what became of them in the minds of the young people listening to him and who, being less tired than him and more true than him to his youth, took his thoughts to their practical conclusion, to the point of conspiracy. After all, Rubashov says to himself, looking at the young man accusing him, perhaps he is the truth of which I was thinking.

Rubashov never recommended terrorism and when he spoke of using violence against the Party leadership, he only meant political violence. But political violence means arrests, and what hap-

---

[2]Hegel, *The Phenomenology of Mind,* London, George Allen and Unwin Ltd., 1949, pp. 642-679.

pens when he who is arrested defends himself? Rubashov was never in the pay of a foreign country. But since he had thought vaguely of overthrowing the Party leadership he should at least have foreseen the reaction of neighboring countries and perhaps to have disarmed it in advance. Thus there was that brief conversation with a foreign diplomat in which no deal was concluded, in which everything was conditional and kept very tentative, but where the price of a friendly neutrality was nevertheless indicated. Of course, to Rubashov it was only a matter of eventually sacrificing a province in order to save the future of the Revolution; but for the foreign diplomat it was a matter of weakening and dismembering the country of the Revolution. Who can say which of the two calculations was right in the end, and whether in the last analysis and before history, Rubashov would have been the savior or the ruin of the Revolution? Moreover, since history is polarized and the dynamics of the class struggle involve the interpretation of every event in favor of one or the other side, there can be no room for neutral or indifferent actions, for even silence plays its role and the shifts between intention and action, self and the other, opposition and treason are unnoticeable. Finally, *once he has been arrested,* Rubashov the opposition member *becomes* in truth a traitor. By the fact of having been beaten, the opposition confesses its inability to establish a new revolutionary leadership. Historically, it amounts to nothing more than an attempt against the only possible revolutionary leadership and thus it becomes counterrevolutionary and treasonable. The results of the attempt work back upon its origins and reveal its total significance.

If Rubashov had wished to invoke his own intentions against this mode of objective thinking, he would have been calling to his aid a philosophy which he had always denied. How could he reject the judgment of the new generation which he had helped to form and which practiced objective thinking to the very limit? After all, it is Rubashov who judges Rubashov through the voice of Gletkin. That is why in the end he will sign the "false" confessions prepared by Gletkin. At first he pleaded guilty of having adopted an *objectively* counterrevolutionary position. It was to be understood that his intentions remained revolutionary. If he let Gletkin "dot the i's" and translate into a conspiracy what was only a self-criticism of the Party and the regime, at least he refused to confess to being a spy and a saboteur.

But this last defense was removed. Revolutionary honor itself is only a species of bourgeois dignity. Rubashov belongs to a generation which believed it could restrict violence to the enemies of the proletariat, treat the proletariat and its representatives humanely, and save one's personal honor through devotion to the Revolution. That is because he and his comrades were intellectuals born in comfortable circumstances and brought up in a prerevolutionary culture. They were eight or nine years old when they were given their first watch. They were unaware that their values presupposed a certain state of freedom and comfort and were completely meaningless apart from it. They had not experienced need and necessity. For himself, Gletkin was sixteen years old when he learned that the hour is divided into sixty minutes. He was born among the peasants who now work in the factories. He knows that they cannot be let free if one wants them to work and that a legal system remains purely nominal as long as its material basis has not been established. Between Rubashov and Gletkin there is the difference between a political generation which by chance had shared the cultural privileges of the bourgeoisie and a generation commissioned to spread culture universally, but first to establish its economic foundations. The distinction between the subjective and the objective, familiar to Rubashov, is however ignored by Gletkin. Gletkin stands for humanity conscious of its material roots; he is the realization of what Rubashov had always spoken. *Objective* sabotage, *objective* treason—intentions notwithstanding—still belongs to the language of an earlier culture or to tomorrow's culture. Under the present circumstances, the inward man no longer exists, or not yet, and thus one can suppress this misleading distinction. One has to surrender.

But Rubashov is not yet finished with himself. While he was speaking before the tribunal, accusing himself and bringing dishonor upon himself, he was still living within history. But there was still the test of the last days in prison to come. He had put himself in order with history, he had concluded his public life just as he had begun it and he had redeemed his past. But, for a while longer, he survived that life which he had already brought to a close. How could he without suppressing his own conscience or without becoming Gletkin, believe himself to have been a traitor and a saboteur? He himself is not universal history; he is Rubashov. He had managed for the last time to surrender himself to history and to look like a traitor to the others, but he could not possibly regard himself in the same way. From the very fact of still being alive, he inevitably judges both his own surrender, since he is the author of it, and the system which demands it. How then does he see his life at this moment? Whether they realized it or not, he and his comrades had started from the affirmation of a value: the value of men. One does not become a revolutionary through science, but out of indignation. Science comes afterward to fill in and delimit that open protest. It taught Rubashov and his companions that the liberation of man presupposed a socialist economy and so they set to work. But he learned that in order to construct this economy in the particular circumstances of the land of the Revolution it was necessary to impose greater suffering than was known under the ancient regime; that in order to free men in the future it was necessary to oppress men in the present. Once the work had begun it established such forceful imperatives that all perspective was lost: "The work had lasted forty years, and right at the start he had forgotten the question for whose sake he had embarked on it."[3] The consciousness of self and the other which had animated the enterprise at the start had become entangled in the web of mediations separating existing humanity from its future fulfillment.

Having done everything that he had had to do, it is not at all surprising that Rubashov is ready to *recover himself* and to yield to that alien and as yet unknown experience for him, which consists in the inner grasp of oneself as consciousness: as a being outside time and space, a light upon which depends every appearance and every conceivable thing, and before which everything that happens, every sorrow and every joy is a matter of indifference—finally, as participation in an infinite. It is before this infinite that at the moment he feels accountable and guilty. Now that history is finished for him, he is following in the reverse direction the road traced by Hegel in the *Phenomenology* from death or from consciousness to History. Should he perhaps have abandoned the attempt to build a new state so as to remain faithful to the actual capacity of humanity? Perhaps it is better to act as a moral man and to bear witness daily to the inward man. "Perhaps it was not suitable for a man to think every

---

[3]*Darkness at Noon*, p. 244.

thought to its logical conclusion."⁴ "Perhaps it did not suit mankind to sail without ballast. And perhaps reason alone was a defective compass, which led one on such a winding, twisted course that the goal finally disappeared in the mist."⁵ Shut up within this internal evidence, and thus disengaged from the world, Rubashov can no longer find any meaning in his behavior during the trial, nor in his death. Is it only now that he sees more clearly—or was it when he was in front of the tribunal? "He was a man who had lost his shadow, free from all impediments. ..."

One may wonder what sense there is in reflecting on history when one no longer has any historical shadow, or in reflecting on life once one is shut out from it. Is it in life or before death that one understands life better? If he were suddenly set free and restored to the Party, how would he continue his life, since while he disposed of it freely and up to the very last moments before the tribunal, he refused to speak in the accents of the inward man? Do Rubashov's last reflections yield us any different a formula for life than that which he followed while alive? Are they not rather the expression of subjectivity's irreducible protestation against an adventure with which it could never be reconciled, but to which it is committed for reasons that are forever valid? Even in his last hours Rubashov does not disavow the Revolution: "Perhaps the Revolution had come too early, an abortion with monstrous deformed limbs. Perhaps the whole thing had been a bad mistake in timing."⁶ And perhaps, once the economic foundations were established, a society would be possible later in which the means would conform to the ends and the individual, instead of being cancelled in favor of the collective interest, would reunite with other individuals to constitute together an earthly infinity.⁷ Even in the closing pages of the book, Koestler therefore does not exactly reach a conclusion. His personal conclusion is to be found elsewhere. *Darkness at Noon* limits itself to the description of a dialectical situation from which Rubashov does not break free even by force of the "oceanic feeling." It is the dialectic created by man's inability to find outside himself

⁴*Ibid.*, p. 247.
⁵*Ibid.*, p. 248.
⁶*Ibid.*, p. 248.
⁷*Ibid.*, p. 249.

what inwardly he senses himself to be, and yet not to keep from looking outside himself for that very thing. Once humanism attempts to fulfill itself with any consistency it becomes transformed into its opposite, namely, into violence.

One is tempted to reply to Koestler that Marxism has actually transcended the alternatives in which Rubashov loses himself. And indeed there is very little Marxism in *Darkness at Noon,* whether in Rubashov's formulas, those of Gletkin, or those of Koestler once one looks into them. The solidarity of the individual with history which Rubashov and his comrades experienced in the revolutionary struggle gets translated into a mechanistic philosophy which disfigures it and is the source of the inhuman alternatives with which Rubashov finishes. To them, man is simply the reflection of his surroundings; the great man is the one whose ideas reflect most exactly the objective conditions of action; and history at least in principle is a rigorous science.

> Perhaps later, much later, it would be taught by means of tables of statistics, supplemented by such anatomical sections. The teacher would draw on the blackboard an algebraic formula representing the conditions of life of the masses of a particular nation at a particular period: "Here, citizens, you see the objective factors which conditioned this process." And, pointing with his ruler to a gray foggy landscape between the second and third lobe of No. I's brain, "Now you see the subjective reflection of these factors"...[8]

In ethics as in philosophy Rubashov and his comrades believed it was necessary to choose between inward and external values; either conscience is everything or else it is nothing:

> There are only two conceptions of human ethics, and they are at opposite poles. One of them is Christian and humane, declares the individual to be sacrosanct, and asserts that the rules of arithmetic are not to be applied to human units. The other starts from the basic principle that a collective aim justifies all means, and not only allows, but demands, that the individual should in every way be subordinated and sacrificed to the community—which may dispose of it as an experimentation rabbit or a sacrificial lamb.[9]

[8]*Ibid.,* pp. 23-24.
[9]*Ibid.,* p. 153.

Here Rubashov and his comrades are following a sort of socio-logical scientism rather than anything in Marx. Political man is an engineer who employs means useful to achieving a given end. The logic which Rubashov follows is not the existential logic of history described by Marx and expressed in the inseparability of objective necessity and *the spontaneous movement of the masses;* it is the summary logic of the technician who deals only with inert objects which he manipulates as he pleases. Given that the goal to be achieved is the power of the proletariat, represented by the Party, individuals are simply the instruments of the Party. "The Party leadership is mistaken," a German militant tells Rubashov after the failure of the German revolution. "The Party can never be mis-taken," said Rubashov. "You and I can make a mistake. Not the Party."[10] This would be a Marxist reply if it meant that resolu-tions taken after discussion are binding because they express the ef-fective state of the Revolution in the world and the way that situation is experienced by the masses, and that consequently, in a Marxist philosophy of history, revolutions are the best possible testimony for the individual. But Rubashov's reply is in no way Marxist if it attributes a divine infallibility to the Party; since the Party has to *deliberate,* there can be no question of any geometric proof or any perfectly clear line. Since there are *detours* it shows that at certain moments the official line needs reconsideration and that if it were persisted in would lead to error.

In Rubashov's mind and in Koestler's version of communism, history is no longer what it was for Marx: the manifestation of human values through a process which might involve dialectical detours but at least could not entirely ignore human purposes. History is no longer the living element of man, the response to his wishes, the locus of revolutionary fraternity. It becomes an external force which has lost the sense of the individual and becomes the sheer force of fact. Hegel's famous saying that "The real is the rational and the rational is the real" is interpreted by Rubashov as an arbitrary justification of everything that exists in the name of a history that knows better than we do where it is going. The same formula did not stop Marx from preserving the role of conscious-ness in the achievement of the revolution and it generally serves

[10]*Ibid.,* pp. 47-48.

Marxists as an invitation to understand the course of events and to modify events through understanding. Instead of the "real" becoming transparent to reason once it is understood, rationality effaces itself before the obscurity of what is real and judgment surrenders to the adoration of an unknown god. "History knows no scruples and no hesitation, inert and unerring, she flows towards her goal. At every bend in her course she leaves the mud which she carries and the corpses of the drowned. History knows her way. She makes no mistakes."[11] Marx himself had written:

> It is not "history" which uses men as a means of achieving—as if it were an individual person—*its* own ends. History is *nothing* but the activity of men in pursuit of their ends.[12]

Evidently, Rubashov knows very well that no one can know anything but fragments of such a thoroughly deterministic History, that for everyone there are lacunae in this objectified History and no one can possess more than a "subjective image" of it which he is in no position to compare with an objectified History conceived as something far transcending humanity. But from the fact that an objectified History means nothing to us Koestler does not conclude that the realist myth should be abandoned. He simply projects it into the future and in the expectation of that happy day when we shall have knowledge of the whole of history, though a rigorous science abandons us to our disagreements and conflicts. It is only in a far-off future that science will be in a position to eliminate the subjective elements in our forecasts and to construct a thoroughly objective model of our relations with history. "Until this stage was reached, politics would remain bloody dilettantism, mere superstition and black magic."[13] This will be a gamble. "Meanwhile he is bound to act on credit and to sell his soul to the devil, in the hope of history's absolution."[14]

Marxism had understood that it is inevitable that our understand-

---

[11]*Ibid.*, p. 48.

[12]*Karl Marx, Selected Writings in Sociology and Social Philosophy.* Edited and with an Introduction and Notes by T. B. Bottomore and M. Rubel, London, Watts & Co., 1956, p. 63.

[13]*Darkness at Noon*, p. 24.

[14]*Ibid.*, p. 99.

ing of history should be partial since every consciousness is itself historically situated. But instead of concluding that we are locked in our subjectivity and sworn to magic as soon as we try to act on the world, Marxism discovered, apart from scientific knowledge and its dream of impersonal truth, a new foundation for historical truth in the spontaneous logic of human existence, in the proletariat's self-recognition and the real development of the revolution. Marxism rested on the profound idea that human perspectives, however relative, are absolute because there is nothing else and no destiny. We grasp the absolute through our total *praxis,* if not through our knowledge — or, rather, men's mutual *praxis* is the absolute. Rubashov has no conception of the wisdom of Marxism, which comes from basing knowledge on *praxis,* which is in turn clarified by knowledge, or from the shaping of the proletariat by theoretical discussion that is in turn subject to the consent of the proletariat. He does not understand the art of the great Marxists of 1917 who deciphered history while it was taking place and projected its trends through decisions that avoided equally any subjective folly or *amor fati.* Rubashov has no other policy or any other interpretation of history with which to challenge the Party leadership; he has only the memory of Arlova, the image of Richard or Little Loewy — emotions, anxieties, and pangs of conscience which never disturb his basic faith in *the wisdom of the event.* But such a trust makes opinions useless and disarms Rubashov before he starts. He does not try to understand history; he simply waits for its judgment in fear and trembling.

> The horror which No. 1 emanated, above all consisted in the possibility that he was in the right....[15]

> And what if, after all, No. 1 were in the right? If here, in dirt and blood and lies, after all and in spite of everything, the grandiose foundations of the future were being laid? Had not history always been an inhumane, unscrupulous builder, mixing its mortar of lies, blood and mud?[16]

> But who will be proved right? It will only be known later.[17]

[15]*Ibid.,* p. 21.
[16]*Ibid.,* p. 126.
[17]*Ibid.,* p. 99.

> There was certainty; only the appeal to that mocking oracle they
> called History, who gave her sentence only when the jaws of the ap
> pealer had long since fallen to dust.[18]

Like any form of masochism, this fascination with death and passion for obedience is ephemeral and ambiguous. Thus it can alternate the passion to command with shamelessly fine sentiments so
that Rubashov is always on the point of switching from one attitude
to the other and is always on the verge of treason. The original
violence, which is the foundation of all other forms of violence, is
that exerted by History when objectified as an incomprehensible
Will before which all individual opinions are compounded as
equally fragile hypotheses. Had Rubashov managed only once to
criticize the notion of an entirely objective and determinate history and realized that the only history we are entitled to speak of
is one whose image and future we ourselves construct by means of
equally methodical and creative interpretations, he would not
have lost sight of the conjectural nature of his and No. 1's opinions;
he might then have escaped the labyrinth of treason and renunciation. Far from lending the individual the supporting weight of
objectivity, the scientistic myth discredits individual analysis in the
name of an ungraspable objective History and merely leaves the
individual oscillating between revolt and passivity.

One passage among all the others in *Darkness at Noon* shows what
little understanding Koestler has of Marxism. It is where, after
going back to his cell, Rubashov begins to explain his confession in
terms of the "theory of the relative maturity of the masses." In a
document addressed to the Central Committee he shows that since
every technical progress makes the operation of the economy unintelligible to the masses, the discussion and democracy which are
possible at a lower level of development become impractical for
some time in a changing economy and can only be restored much
later when the masses have caught up with the intervening changes
and the objective conditions of production. Whereas in a period of
relative maturity it is the legitimate task of the opposition to debate
and appeal to the masses, in a period of relative immaturity, it
should simply toe the line. It is clear what Koestler thinks of such
reasoning. He cites alongside it Machiavelli's teaching that words

[18]*Ibid.*, p. 22.

serve to disguise deeds, to excuse the disguise once it is discovered, in addition to the famous saying from the Gospels according to which the Christian should say *"Yea"* or *"Nay,"* anything else added being only the work of the devil. But this is to imply that Rubashov is systematically lying and afterward inventing good reasons for himself. It is also evidence that Marxist problems are not very well understood. The Marxist has recognized the mystification involved in the inner life; he lives in the world and in history. As he sees it, decision is not a private matter, it is not the spontaneous affirmation of those values we favor; rather, it consists in questioning our situation in the world, inserting ourselves in the course of events, in properly understanding and expressing the movement of history outside of which values remain empty words and have no other chance of realization. The difference between the adventurer who covers his retraction with theoretical pretexts and the Marxist who bases his commitment on a general thesis is that the former sets himself in the center of the world while the latter does not want to live outside of an intersubjective truth. Back in prison Rubashov constructs the theory of his confession with no dishonor to himself because his confession has its roots in the general situation of the home of the Revolution as he has reviewed in his conversation with Ivanov. All that might be said to Rubashov is that even this "objective" view of the historical situation is still one which he has endorsed; the individual cannot suppress the necessity of choosing, and even when he believes he is responding to what history expects of him, it is still he who interprets this expectation so that he can never displace his own responsibility; his view of the situation always involves the risk of error and partiality, so there is always the question of knowing whether he constructed his theory to make his peace with the Party because he found it hard to be alone.

Had Koestler limited himself to saying that there is a permanent risk of illusion and cowardice in any behavior which is based on the exigencies of the objective situation instead of on the abstract imperatives of subjective morality, there would have been something in what he says. But that would not constitute any condemnation of Marxism or any rehabilitation of moralism and the "beautiful soul." All one would have to reply is that, that is the way things are, human life is lived like this; Marxism expresses these facts and is not the cause of them; despite everything, we have to work without certainty and in confusion to uncover a truth. To confront Rubashov with the Christian absolute "Yea" or "Nay," or Kant's moral imperative, simply shows that one refuses to face the problem and falls back upon the attitudes of the holy will and the pharisee. It is necessary from the start to recognize *as a moral claim* the Communist's preoccupation with the role of objective factors and his wish to look upon himself from a standpoint both within and outside of history. One only has the right to point out the risks of "objective morality" if one also points out those of an ostentatious "subjective morality." In this instance, as in so many others, Koestler poses the problem in pre-Marxist terms. Marxism is neither the negation of subjectivity and human action nor the scientistic materialism with which Rubashov began. It is much more a theory of concrete subjectivity and concrete action—of subjectivity and action committed within a historical situation. Rubashov thinks he has discovered a mortal contradiction in the heart of Communist thought on fatalism and revolution.

> The individual stood under the sign of economic fatality, a wheel in a clockwork which had been wound up for all eternity and could not be stopped or influenced—and the Party demanded that the wheel should revolt against the clockwork and change its course.[19]

But who said that history is a clockwork and the individual a wheel? It was not Marx; it was Koestler. It is strange that in Koestler there is no inkling of the commonplace notion that by the very fact of its duration, history sketches the outline for the transformation of its own structures, changing and reversing its own direction because, in the last analysis men come to collide with the structures that alienate them inasmuch as economic man is also a human being. In short, Koestler has never given much thought to the simple idea of a dialectic in history.

However, the fact that Koestler is a mediocre Marxist does not release us from his questions: on the contrary, it raises them all the more sharply. Whatever the position in theoretical Marxism, Koestler the Communist sees in History an unfathomable God, overlooks the individual, and is unaware of the permutation of subjective and objective factors which is the key to the great Marxists. But Koestler's

[19]*Ibid.*, p. 246.

case is not rare; scientistic and objectivistic deviations are quite frequent. Even if the alternatives of subjectivism and objectivism are resolved in Marx's Marxism, the question still remains whether this is so in communism as a reality and whether the majority of Communists believe in incorporating subjectivity, or whether like Koestler they prefer to deny it in theory and practice. Even the mistakes that Koestler makes in his formulation of the problems leads us to the following questions: Is there in reality any alternative between efficacy and humanity, between historical action and morality? Is it true that we have to choose between being a Commissar—working for men from the outside, treating them as instruments—or being a Yogi—that is, calling men to a completely inward reform? Is it true that revolutionary power negates the individual, his judgment, his intentions, his honor, and even his revolutionary honor? Is it true that in the face of a revolutionary power and a world polarized by the class struggle there are only two possible positions: absolute docility or treason? Is it true, finally, that, in the famous saying of Napoleon, politics is the modern tragedy in which the truth of the individual confronts the demands of the collectivity, as the will of the hero in Greek tragedies confronted a destiny determined by the gods? Claude Morgan wrote that *Darkness at Noon* is the work of a *provocateur,* meaning that Koestler blackens revolutionary action the better to discredit it, and invented his soul-destroying dilemmas arbitrarily. But is Rubashov nothing more than a fictional character and are his problems simply imaginary ones?

The Roads to Communism and Back

by Rebecca West

There is no subject on which it is more difficult to establish communication with one's fellow creatures than anti-communism; and here the gulf yawns particularly wide between Europeans and Americans. Europeans steeped in political activities of a minor sort according to the habit of their kind may speak of Communists with the tart exasperation which comes of frustrating experience. Without number are the ways they may have been done in the eye by the comrades, and all are disagreeable.

For example, take the case of a member of the Labor party who has worked for a Labor candidate and seen him returned to Parliament, only to find that the constituency suddenly becomes riddled with ostensibly Labor activities which turn out to be, in effect, hostile to the Labor Government and to this particular member of Parliament; and it turns out that the promoter of these activities is none other than the candidate's election agent, who proves to be a member of the Communist party, though before he was admitted to the Labor party he had signed a declaration that he was not a Communist. Nobody likes to be told lies or to be cheated and a community would be in a poor way when it lost this instinctive reaction.

Europeans smarting from such experiences are apt to be indignant and impatient when they allude to communism as a pernicious nuisance and are looked at by their listeners as if their slips were showing. The idea, which has been successfully put over in some quarters, that anti-communism is dowdy seems to them cheap and frivolous. But equally, they feel repelled by the kind of sympathy they may involuntarily attract.

They have no desire to hold hands with their afflicted brothers and sisters who think that Russians are putting poison in their food; or who wish to suspend the protection given to all citizens by law in the case of suspected or proven Communists; or who want to make war on the airy off-chance that it may prevent another one. Above all, they do not want to be linked with people who hope to freeze the social system in its present state and so perpetuate injustice and cruelty. They are indeed anti-Communist because they believe Communists are one of the chief forces which prevent the transformation of the world into a commonwealth.

This book of essays,[1] by four former members of the Communist party and two one-time friends of the party (André Gide and Louis Fischer), tells that European story. It is true that two of the essays are by Americans (Mr. Fischer and Richard Wright) and one of those describes an American situation; and that essay by Richard Wright is most moving of all. But the others relate to this specifically European exasperation which so often becomes tongue-tied when it ought to justify itself. One of them, indeed, may become a classic by reason of its subtle and candid and comprehensive statement of this typical experience of this age.

Arthur Koestler's essay is one of the most handsome presents that has ever been given to future historians of our time. He is, of course, always an interesting writer. His work is three-dimensional because he is three people. In him there is a believing poet who perpetually changes into an unbelieving critic savagely eager to tear up all evidence of his previous manifestations of faith but never able to complete the work of destruction before he changes back into the poet who is equally eager to fill the wastepaper basket with all evidences of the critic's skepticism; while another part of him, as tough and jaunty as a racetrack gambler, looks over the wall at this protean struggle quite unimpressed and comments on it with ribald wit. Here he recreates the most formative experience of his life, analyzes it, mocks it.

At 26 he was in Berlin working in the great liberal and anti-militarist publishing house of Ullstein. He was an old 26. Up till the age of 9 he had lived in the sort of cushioned and cultured home that was maintained by the Jewish mercantile class in Hungary. Then his father, who was an agent for British and German textiles, was reduced to poverty by World War I and was finally rendered

---

[1]*The God That Failed: A Confession.* New York: Harper and Row Co., 1950.

completely destitute by the Austrian inflation of the early Twenties. At 21 Arthur Koestler left home to become the sole financial support of his parents.

Now he had established himself firmly in a community that had nothing firm about it. Around him stretched the peculiar panorama of the Weimar Republic in its last days: such a tatty and disordered landscape with here and there a vast undertaking (such as Ullstein's) looming up in unquestionable magnificence; such an infantile population that while a trumpet of doom echoed from the skies formed itself into a cops-and-robber game from which individual players sometimes detached themselves to engage in artistic intellectual achievement not to be surpassed in any other country.

He undertook to support this tottering civilization as he had taken on the care of his parents and to that end he joined the Communist party. Membership never came easy to him. The poet was scandalized by party jargon which stultified thought. The critic had to blink before he could swallow the policy forced on German Communists by Moscow, which, as he shows in some of the most interesting pages of this essay, never missed a trick in helping Hitler to power; the puerilities by which the Communists split the progressive vote and let the Nazis in will seem incredible if it is not borne in mind by the reader that the U.S.S.R. radio was every day blaring out its conviction that the threat to European peace lay in the armed might and the imperialist philosophy of France.

Also, the ribald part of Mr. Koestler was greatly amused by such naïveté as that of the Communist propaganda chief who, to keep his mind pure, only read the official party organ.

Certainly Mr. Koestler noticed all these follies: for he can now recall his strangulated doubts regarding them. But he noticed them only as a partially anesthetized patient notices what is going on in his sickroom, and the name of the anesthetic was contentment. There is no doubt that this supremely gifted man found deep satisfaction, greater perhaps than any he has ever found elsewhere, in Communist party membership.

Obviously, one reason for this lay in the relief felt by a man who after having been overburdened with responsibility since his childhood surrenders his will to a powerful organization. But also it was a way of life which promised full employment to both body and soul in a world where unemployment in the sense of the inability of the body to work and the soul to believe was a constant overhanging danger. Perhaps the party's strongest card was that it pleased pride by demanding constant self-sacrifice beyond the point of enduring poverty and life on the run to prison cell and gallows.

Mr. Koestler is frank about the rewards that are open to the Communist writer; he gives an illuminating account of his journey through Soviet Russia in 1932, when eight of ten local state publishing trusts bought the rights of the same short story (always at something well over ten times the monthly salary of an average Soviet wage earner) and paid him advances on the Russian, German, Ukrainian, Georgian and Armenian rights of his unwritten book on the Soviet Union "which amounted to a small fortune." At that time he had not published a single book.

But it was plainly not this baksheesh that won him. It was working on that anti-Fascist propaganda for ten to twelve hours a day unpaid, with little food but a dish of thick pea soup at noon and walking several miles a day to the only free lodging he could find—a hayloft.

He liked best of all his service in the Spanish Civil War, which ended for him in four months in Spanish prisons, most of the time in solitary confinement and in expectation of being shot. There he found a peaceful ecstasy. Nevertheless, he left the Communist party which had given him all these experiences. It was so great a wrench that he has plainly felt himself a maimed man ever since.

But it had been part of the revelation he had received in prison to discover "that the end justifies the means only within very narrow limits, that ethics is not a function of social utility and charity not a petty bourgeois sentiment but a gravitational force which keeps civilization in its orbit." This forbade him to pretend that the members of POUM, the Trotskyite splinter group that was participating in the Spanish Civil War, were traitors and agents of Franco, as the Communist party line pretended.

It made him suddenly revolt against purges and fight for the lives of two friends who were suddenly arrested on fantastic charges after having spent their lives in the service of the Soviet Union. Of this he writes bitterly, accusing all Communists and fellow travelers of participation in blood-guilt:

> Every single one of us knows of at least one friend who perished in the Arctic subcontinent of forced labor camps, was shot as a spy or vanished without trace. How our voices boomed with righteous

indignation, denouncing flaws in the procedure of justice in our comfortable democracies; and how silent we were when our comrades, without trial or conviction, were liquidated in the Socialist sixth of the earth. Each of us carries a skeleton in the cupboard of his conscience; added together, they would form galleries of bones more labyrinthine than the Paris catacombs.

The Ribbentrop-Molotov pact severed the last shred of his contact with communism. He had given seven years of his life to the party and it was his conviction that every moment of these years had been wasted. The means employed by the party only served to extend the sphere of those means. They never brought the ostensible end any nearer.

This story of the dissipation of vital energy on an intricate and useless technique is retold by the novelist Ignazio Silone, whose contribution includes a most interesting account of a Comintern meeting in 1927, where Stalin and Thälmann and Kuusinen and Kolarov wasted time and force on attempting to get him and two non-Russian colleagues to pass a resolution condemning a document by Trotsky which nobody but the Russians had read, a resolution which could by no conceivable process have the smallest practical effect.

The same story is retold again by Richard Wright, though he almost steps out of the volume by reason of his preoccupation with people just as people. This beautiful writer uses a bare style, but the men and women in his pages are there in their flesh; the economical dialogue is delivered in their several and unique voices.

It is retold again by the poet Stephen Spender in an essay which seems more hesitant and diffuse than others, but which contains pictures of intellectuals in the British Communist party so lively that they make Mr. Koestler seem a gentle soul. Here, too, is a most serious discussion of the moral consequences of a bigotry which is repelled by atrocities only when they are committed by the opposition. ("It was clear to me that unless I cared about every murdered child impartially, I did not really care about children being murdered at all. I was performing an obscene mental act on certain corpses which became the fuel for propagandist passions....")

Mr. Spender debates with extreme seriousness and intelligence the problem of what the anti-Communist should do to make his faith positive. He sees that the people and nations who love liberty must "lead a movement throughout the world to improve the conditions of the millions of people who care more for bread than for freedom, thus raising them to a level of existence where they can care for freedom."

At times the essayists seem to claim too much for themselves. Richard Crossman, assistant editor of *The New Statesman and Nation,* whose happy idea it was to compile this volume, and Mr. Koestler both arrive at the conclusion that people who are most likely to set the world at rights are ex-Communists, on the theory that one who has descended into hell will thirst all the more for heaven. But this is disproved here by the only platitudinous essay in the book: André Gide's enthusiasm for communism seems to have been a superficial experience and his disenchantment with it no more profound.

It must be remembered that all the writers of these essays, with the exception of Richard Wright, could have learned from others what they had learned for themselves about communism. The information was already available, and some lack of shrewdness, some masochistic urge must have led them to disregard it.

The value of this book is not that its authors showed themselves outstanding, but that they were typical. It is a truly contemporary book; it shows how at the moment Europeans of this kind regard communism.

The Ex-Communist's Conscience

by Isaac Deutscher

Ignazio Silone relates that he once said jokingly to Togliatti, the Italian Communist leader: "The final struggle will be between the communists and the ex-communists." There is a bitter drop of truth in the joke. In the propaganda skirmishes against the U.S.S.R. and communism, the ex-Communist or the ex-fellow traveler is the most active sharpshooter. With the peevishness that distinguishes him from Silone, Arthur Koestler makes a similar point: "It's the same with all you comfortable, insular, Anglo-Saxon anti-communists. You hate our Cassandra cries and resent us as allies — but, when all is said, we ex-communists are the only people on your side who know what it's all about."

The ex-Communist is the problem child of contemporary politics. He crops up in the oddest places and corners. He buttonholes you in Berlin to tell the story of *his* "battle of Stalingrad," fought here, in Berlin, against Stalin. You find him in de Gaulle's entourage: none other than André Malraux, the author of *Man's Fate*. In America's strangest political trial the ex-Communist has, for months, pointed his finger at Alger Hiss. Another ex-Communist, Ruth Fischer, denounces her brother, Gerhart Eisler, and castigates the British for not having handed him back to the United States. An ex-Trotskyite, James Burnham, flays the American businessman for his real or illusory lack of capitalist class consciousness, and sketches a program of action for nothing less than the world-wide defeat of communism. And now six writers — Koestler, Silone, André Gide, Louis Fischer, Richard Wright, and Stephen Spender — get together to expose and destroy *The God That Failed*.

"The Ex-Communist's Conscience." From *Heretics and Renegades* (original title: *Russia in Transition*) by Isaac Deutscher. First published in the United States by Coward, McCann Inc., 1957, and in England by Jonathan Cape Ltd., 1957; reissued in the United States by The Bobbs-Merrill Co., Inc., 1969. Reprinted by permission of the Executors of the Isaac Deutscher Estate.

The "legion" of ex-Communists does not march in close formation. It is scattered far and wide. Its members resemble one another very much, but they also differ. They have common traits and individual features. All have left an army and a camp—some as conscientious objectors, some as deserters, and others as marauders. A few stick quietly to their conscientious objections, while others vociferously claim commissions in an army which they had bitterly opposed. All wear threadbare bits and pieces of the old uniform, supplemented by the quaintest new rags. And all carry with them their common resentments and individual reminiscences.

Some joined the party at one time, others at another; the date of joining is relevant to their further experiences. Those, for instance, who joined in the 1920's went into a movement in which there was plenty of scope for revolutionary idealism. The structure of the party was still fluid; it had not yet gone into the totalitarian mold. Intellectual integrity was still valued in a Communist; it had not yet been surrendered for good to Moscow's *raison d'état*. Those who joined the party in the 1930's began their experience on a much lower level. Right from the beginning they were manipulated like recruits on the party's barrack squares by the party's sergeant majors.

This difference bears upon the quality of the ex-Communist's reminiscences. Silone, who joined the party in 1921, recalls with real warmth his first contact with it; he conveys fully the intellectual excitement and moral enthusiasm with which communism pulsated in those early days. The reminiscences of Koestler and Spender, who joined in the 1930's, reveal the utter moral and intellectual sterility of the party's first impact on them. Silone and his comrades were intensely concerned with fundamental ideas before and after they became absorbed in the drudgery of day-to-day duty. In Koestler's story, his party "assignment," right from the first moment, overshadows all matters of personal conviction and ideal. The Communist of the early drafts was a revolutionary before he became, or was expected to become, a puppet. The Communist of the later drafts hardly got the chance to breathe the genuine air of revolution.

Nevertheless, the original motives for joining were similar, if not identical, in almost every case: experience of social injustice or degradation; a sense of insecurity bred by slumps and social crises; and the craving for a great ideal or purpose, or for a reliable intel lectual guide through the shaky labyrinth of modern society. The newcomer felt the miseries of the old capitalist order to be unbearable; and the glowing light of the Russian revolution illumined those miseries with extraordinary sharpness.

Socialism, classless society, the withering away of the State—all seemed around the corner. Few of the newcomers had any premonition of the blood and sweat and tears to come. To himself, the intellectual convert to communism seemed a new Prometheus—except that he would not be pinned to the rock by Zeus's wrath. "Nothing henceforth [so Koestler now recalls his own mood in those days] can disturb the convert's inner peace and serenity—except the occasional fear of losing faith again...."

... There can be no greater tragedy than that of a great revolution's succumbing to the mailed fist that was to defend it from its enemies. There can be no spectacle as disgusting as that of a post-revolutionary tyranny dressed up in the banners of liberty. The ex-Communist is morally as justified as was the ex-Jacobin in revealing and revolting against that spectacle.

But is it true, as Koestler claims, that "ex-Communists are the only people...who know what it's all about?" One may risk the assertion that the exact opposite is true: Of all people, the ex-Communists know least what it is all about.

At any rate, the pedagogical pretensions of ex-Communist men of letters seem grossly exaggerated. Most of them (Silone is a notable exception) have never been inside the real Communist movement, in the thick of its clandestine or open organization. As a rule, they moved on the literary or journalistic fringe of the party. Their notions of Communist doctrine and ideology usually spring from their own literary intuition, which is sometimes acute but often misleading.

Worse still is the ex-Communist's characteristic incapacity for detachment. His emotional reaction against his former environment keeps him in its deadly grip and prevents him from understanding the drama in which he was involved or half-involved. The picture of communism and Stalinism he draws is that of a gigantic chamber of intellectual and moral horrors. Viewing it, the uninitiated are transferred from politics to pure demonology. Sometimes the artistic effect may be strong—horrors and demons do enter into many a poetic masterpiece; but it is politically unreliable and even dangerous. Of course, the story of Stalinism abounds in horror. But this is only one of its elements; and even this, the demonic, has to be translated into terms of human motives and interests. The ex-Communist does not even attempt the translation.

In a rare flash of genuine self-criticism, Koestler makes this admission:

> As a rule, our memories romanticize the past. But when one has renounced a creed or been betrayed by a friend, the opposite mechanism sets to work. In the light of that later knowledge, the original experience loses its innocence, becomes tainted and rancid in recollection. I have tried in these pages to recapture the mood in which the experiences [in the Communist Party] related were originally lived—and I know that I have failed. Irony, anger, and shame kept intruding; the passions of that time seem transformed into perversions, its inner certitude into the closed universe of the drug addict; the shadow of barbed wire lies across the condemned playground of memory. Those who were caught by the great illusion of our time, and have lived through its moral and intellectual debauch, either give themselves up to a new addiction of the opposite type, or are condemned to pay with a lifelong hangover.

This need not be true of all ex-Communists. Some may still feel that their experience has been free from the morbid overtones described by Koestler. Nevertheless, Koestler has given here a truthful and honest characterization of the type of ex-Communist to which he himself belongs. But it is difficult to square this self-portrait with his other claim that the confraternity for which he speaks "are the only people…who know what it's all about." With equal right a sufferer from traumatic shock might claim that he is the only one who really understands wounds and surgery. The most that the intellectual ex-Communist knows, or rather feels, is his own sickness; but he is ignorant of the nature of the external violence that has produced it, let alone the cure.

This irrational emotionalism dominates the evolution of many an ex-Communist. "The logic of opposition at all cost," says Silone, "has carried many ex-communists far from their starting-points, in some cases as far as fascism." What were those starting-points? Nearly every ex-Communist broke with his party in the name of communism. Nearly every one set out to defend the ideal of socialism from the abuses of a bureaucracy subservient to Moscow. Nearly every one began by throwing out the dirty water of the Russian revolution to protect the baby bathing in it.

Sooner or later these intentions are forgotten or abandoned. Having broken with a party bureaucracy in the name of communism, the heretic goes on to break with communism itself. He claims to have made the discovery that the root of the evil goes far deeper than he at first imagined, even though his digging for that "root" may have been very lazy and very shallow. He no longer defends socialism from unscrupulous abuse; he now defends mankind from the fallacy of socialism. He no longer throws out the dirty water of the Russian revolution to protect the baby; he discovers that the baby is a monster which must be strangled. The heretic becomes a renegade.

How far he departed from his starting-point, whether, as Silone says, he becomes a fascist or not, depends on his inclinations and tastes — and stupid Stalinist heresy-hunting often drives the ex-Communist to extremes. But, whatever the shades of individual attitudes, as a rule the intellectual ex-Communist ceases to oppose capitalism. Often he rallies to its defense, and he brings to this job the lack of scruple, the narrow-mindedness, the disregard for truth, and the intense hatred with which Stalinism has imbued him. He remains a sectarian. He is an inverted Stalinist. He continues to see the world in white and black, but now the colors are differently distributed. As a Communist he saw no difference between fascists and social democrats. As an anti-Communist he sees no difference between nazism and communism. Once, he accepted the party's claim to infallibility; now he believes himself to be infallible. Having once been caught by the "greatest illusion," he is now obsessed by the greatest disillusionment of our time....

"Far, far more abject is thy enemy" might have been the text for *The God That Failed,* and for the philosophy of the lesser evil expounded in its pages. The ardor with which the writers of this book defend the West against Russia and communism is sometimes chilled by uncertainty or residual ideological inhibition. The uncertainty appears between the lines of their confessions, or in curious asides.

Silone, for instance, still describes the pre-Mussolini Italy, against which, as a Communist, he had rebelled, as "pseudo-democratic." He hardly believes that post-Mussolini Italy is any better, but he sees its Stalinist enemy to be "far, far more abject." More than the other co-authors of this book, Silone is surely aware of the price that Europeans of his generation have already paid for the acceptance of lesser-evil philosophies. Louis Fischer advocates the "double rejection" of communism and capitalism, but his rejection of the latter sounds like a feeble face-saving formula; and his newly found cult of Gandhiism impresses one as merely an awkward escapism. But it is Koestler who, occasionally, in the midst of all his affectation and anti-Communist frenzy, reveals a few curious mental reservations: "...if we survey history [he says] and compare the lofty aims, in the name of which revolutions were started, and the sorry end to which they came, we see again and again how a *polluted civilization pollutes its own revolutionary offspring*" (my italics). Has Koestler thought out the implications of his own words, or is he merely throwing out a *bon mot?* If the "revolutionary offspring," communism, has really been "polluted" by the civilization against which it has rebelled, then no matter how repulsive the offspring may be, the source of the evil is not in it but in that civilization. And this will be so regardless of how zealously Koestler himself may act as the advocate of the "defenders" of civilization *à la* Chambers.

Even more startling is another thought—or is this perhaps also only a *bon mot?*—with which Koestler unexpectedly ends his confession:

> I served the Communist Party for seven years—the same length of time as Jacob tended Laban's sheep to win Rachel his daughter. When the time was up, the bride was led into his dark tent; only the next morning did he discover that his ardors had been spent not on the lovely Rachel but on the ugly Leah.
>
> I wonder whether he ever recovered from the shock of having slept with an illusion. I wonder whether afterwards he believed that he had ever believed in it. I wonder whether the happy end of the legend will be repeated; for at the price of another seven years of labor, Jacob was given Rachel too, and the illusion became flesh.
>
> And the seven years seemed unto him but a few days, for the love he had for her.

One might think that Jacob-Koestler reflects uneasily whether he has not too hastily ceased tending Laban-Stalin's sheep, instead of waiting patiently till his "illusion became flesh."

The words are not meant to blame, let alone to castigate, anybody. Their purpose, let this be repeated, is to throw into relief a
confusion of ideas, from which the ex-Communist intellectual is
not the only sufferer.

In one of his recent articles, Koestler vented his irritation at those
good old liberals who were shocked by the excess of anti-Communist
zeal in the former Communist, and viewed him with the disgust
with which ordinary people look at "a defrocked priest taking out
a girl to a dance."

Well, the good old liberals may be right, after all: this peculiar
type of anti-Communist may appear to them like a defrocked priest
"taking out," not just a girl, but a harlot. The ex-Communist's utter
confusion of intellect and emotion makes him ill-suited for any
political activity. He is haunted by a vague sense that he has betrayed either his former ideals or the ideals of bourgeois society;
like Koestler, he may even have an ambivalent notion that he has
betrayed both. He then tries to suppress his sense of guilt and
uncertainty, or to camouflage it by a show of extraordinary certi-
tude and frantic aggressiveness. He insists that the world should
recognize his uneasy conscience as the clearest conscience of all.
He may no longer be concerned with any cause except one—self-
justification. And this is the most dangerous motive for any political activity.

It seems that the only dignified attitude the intellectual ex-Communist can take is to rise *au-dessus de la mêlée.* He cannot join the
Stalinist camp or the anti-Stalinist Holy Alliance without doing
violence to his better self. So let him stay outside any camp. Let him
try to regain critical sense and intellectual detachment. Let him
overcome the cheap ambition to have a finger in the political pie.
Let him be at peace with his own self at least, if the price he has to
pay for phony peace with the world is self-renunciation and self-
denunciation. This is not to say that the ex-Communist man of
letters, or intellectual at large, should retire into the ivory tower.
(His contempt for the ivory tower lingers in him from his past.)
But he may withdraw into a *watchtower* instead. To watch with detachment and alertness this heaving chaos of a world, to be on a
sharp lookout for what is going to emerge from it, and to interpret it
sine ira et studio—this is now the only honorable service the ex-

Communist intellectual can render to a generation in which scrupulous observation and honest interpretation have become so sadly rare. (Is it not striking how little observation and interpretation, and how much philosophizing and sermonizing, one finds in the books of the gifted pleiad of ex-Communist writers?)...

In Search of Penitence

by Stephen Spender

At the age of 47, Arthur Koestler has a crowded life to look back on, fuller than that of most octogenarians. This, the first volume of his autobiography, breaking off with the day when he entered the Communist party, deals only with what Bernard Shaw would call his "nonage." Yet from his origins in Budapest, it takes him to Vienna, Palestine, the Middle East, Berlin, and almost to the North Pole. The next volume will doubtless cover his activities in Russia as a Communist party member, his imprisonment in Malaga by Francoists during the Spanish Civil War, his internment in France in 1940, and his experiences as a member of the Pioneer Corps in England.

Arrow in the Blue, by its references and quotations, reminds us that Mr. Koestler is the author of a number of books which have given him reputations as varied as the different passports he has enjoyed when he has, at various times, settled chameleon-like in some new country. *The Gladiators* promised him a future as a writer of historical fiction; his second, and most famous novel, *Darkness at Noon,* posed the central conflict of the political conscience of our time: the terrible awakening of a mind, aware of the necessity of social revolution in the modern world, to the methods of that revolution in the hands of the Stalinist dictatorship. *Dialogue with Death,* containing portions of his *Spanish Testament* (published in England in 1938) and *Scum of the Earth* are *témoignages* of the Nineteen Thirties and Forties, perhaps the best (because written out of the agonizing experience of events) of their decades.

In *Arrival and Departure* and *The Age of Longing*, there are signs of softening of moral purpose combined with an increased brittleness of feeling, disturbing to Mr. Koestler's admirers. The idea that the "situation of our time" for the man of intelligence and moral feeling is that of the "crusader without a cross" is really self-exploitation of Mr. Koestler's own situation.

The present autobiography opens with a picture of an older Koestler leafing through *The London Times* of Sept. 5, 1905, in search of what he calls his "secular horoscope." He finds a news item describing the burial of a peasant woman—evidently the victim of a pogrom—in Kishinev. Mr. Koestler comments: "It sounded to me like the tuning of an orchestra just before the conductor lifts his wand."

This rather far-sought sign of the night above the cradle of the Koestler babe may not strike the reader as in the best of taste. Yet Mr. Koestler is little concerned with questions of delicacy, and the symbol he has discovered reminds us that he is a new kind of writer —very significant of our time—who has tried to make art out of the events which are generally thought of as the material of journalism.

Ever since his birth he has lived as it were in the maelstrom of contemporary history, turning in a continual vortex even as he wrote, and with an unerring instinct homing toward the place of trouble which will affect us all very soon. His environment is the whirlpool, and his creativity explodes out of violence.

His virtue, however, is not just restlessness and love of the vortex of contemporary history. It lies in his capacity for entering into what I can only call the conscience of contemporary events. That this is a shifting conscience, which tells him at one time to be on one side or at one place and another at a quite different one, is disconcerting and bitter to his political allies, but it is what really makes for his significance as a man and a writer. Mr. Koestler is a restless instrument who attaches himself to a conflict and gives us a kind of reading of the moral issues involved. He reminds us that the reading may be different at different times. Communism was a better cause in 1933 than it is in 1952.

He also has his own personal problem, which is to discover some center within himself which is not shifting, to which he can attach his values and his faith. His danger is to make a heroic virtue out of the changeability which has made him a public success. The weakness of the present book is that he still seems to regard ruthless, analytic honesty as the supreme virtue. When applied to his own personality his rather mechanical self-analysis tends to wither up what is good, and to overemphasize what is erroneous. He analyzes the bad, but he tends to analyze *away* the good by explaining it in terms of more or less pathological motives.

What is best in him is genuine moral indignation (which he treats here as a kind of illness), a passionate self-identification with the underdog and an infectious love of adventure.

Apart from those passages in which Mr. Koestler almost deliberately alienates the reader's sympathy, *Arrow in the Blue* has many excellent things to amuse and satisfy the most varied tastes. There is his childhood in Budapest, his education as a Jewish student in a Jewish students' corps at Vienna University, his pioneering in a communal settlement in Palestine, and his descent into starvation and vagabondage in Jerusalem and Haifa, when he had given up trying to be a settler.

There follows his early success story, when he became employed by the great publishing firm of Ullstein, first as a correspondent and reporter, later as science editor. This he regards as the least sympathetic phase of his own career, and perhaps his hatred of this period of his life casts an inhuman shadow over this volume.

The book ends with one of the best and most exhilarating pieces which Mr. Koestler has written. In holiday mood, he describes with humor and poetry his flight toward the North Pole as the one journalist accompanying Eckener in the most sensational of the trips made by the *Graf Zeppelin*. Apart from some childhood scenes, this is the most likable and probably the best written chapter of this book. Of his ideas, the most important one here, is his first grasp of socialism and its development into Communist ideology. He is always trenchant when he is analyzing communism, but perhaps even more important is his invocation of the idealism and generosity of his first impulse toward the movement which was going to transform the world into a place of enormous prosperity shared by all.

The basic defect of the book is that it is theory-ridden. Not only is it stuffed with ideas which have featured in Mr. Koestler's other books—about Palestine, communism, yogis and commissars and so forth—but also there is a theory as to why Mr. Koestler's mind is laid as wide open to ideologies as his father's was to inventions. The explanation is implicit in his title, *Arrow in the Blue*. In a passage from which this title derives, he describes how, looking up at the sky from a slope near Buda one summer day, it occurred to him that:

> You could shoot a super-arrow into the blue with a super-force which would carry it beyond the earth's gravity, past the moon, past the sun's attraction…and on…and on…. there would be nothing to stop it. My obsession with the arrow was merely the first phase of my quest. When it proved sterile, the infinite as target was replaced by Utopias of one kind or another. It was the same quest and the same all-or-nothing mentality which drove me to the Holy Land and into the Communist party.

Mr. Koestler dissects autobiography into what he calls the "Chronicler's Urge" and the "Ecce Homo" motive. On the one hand, the autobiographer wishes to relate his *témoignage* of the history of his time; on the other, he wishes to reveal his own personality. He lists traps into which previous autobiographers have fallen: the Nostalgic Fallacy of overromanticizing childhood, the Dull Dog Fallacy of portraying himself as a stupid spectator, and so on. Perhaps he is unfair to nostalgia: sometimes it is a gateway which enables a reader to enter an enchanted garden. It is a pity, too, that he did not put in his own particular Fallacy, which is of thinking that life can be caught within categories and divided among catchwords.

With all these precautions, his book alternates between a narrative of events in which he has participated and passages of self-analysis. Whether as narrator or autopsychologist, the analytic method always triumphs. The reader may feel that Mr. Koestler has altogether too much confidence in a science which is often perilously close to science-fiction, and that he has an almost fatal gift for minting cliches. Since he is certainly at his most trenchant when attacking analytic systems like those of Marx and Freud, it seems strange that he has such confidence in the pattern-fabricating method of describing behavior.

At moments one suspects that Mr. Koestler thinks that a pattern of behavior is the same as an existence, just as he appears to think that the pursuit of a goal is the same as attaining one, and that the "search for principles of law and order in the universe" is "an essentially religious endeavor" (in a passage written to prove that scientists are religious). Nor would it occur to him that one of his most quoted phrases—"Crusader without a Cross"—is strictly meaningless, since a crusader without a cross would not be a crusader. He would be a tourist. The infinity into which the super-arrow is directed by a super-force is a super-vacuum. Nor can any other human being fill this vacuum.

Alexander Pope, who was a clever man, wrote that the "proper study of mankind is man," and all the literary artists in the world —excepting Mr. Koestler—have, I think, agreed with him. The religious, the artists, the poets and the novelists have written about human beings in order to discover a point within human behavior where it acquires an indefinable essence of being, a mystery of life To Mr. Koestler, though, the pattern is everything, and when he has explained it away the essence has evaporated.

The problem raised by the Koestler pattern of analysis is that it has the effect first of schematizing the behavior of other people until they appear mere abstractions, and lastly (it would seem, from this book) of making Mr. Koestler himself appear entirely "predictable" to the reader, with the result that his real personality disappears into the brick-work patterning, like the Cheshire cat.

Mr. Koestler can only be said to achieve vitality in these pages when he forgets himself: for instance when, disregarding his own principles, he lavishes pity on poor little Arthur in the doctor's surgery, or when he escapes to the North Pole in the Graf Zeppelin. Apart from this, he has mechanical drive when he is attacking systems as materialist as his own way of thinking: the chapters on Marxism are trenchantly destructive. There are many things to admire in this readable and often irritating autobiography: Mr. Koestler is penetrating, acute, humorous, fearless, adventurous and often amusing. What he lacks is simply the element of love and this makes his own personality seem a blank in the story of his life.

II

"At this point ends this typical case history of a member of the Central European educated middle classes, born in the first years of our century." The more I think about it, the juster appears this paradoxical seeming conclusion of this second and final volume of Koestler's autobiography, covering the years from 1931 to the present. The bitter truth of the matter is that the one thing in which Koestler is not typical is in being alive. What he represents is the millions of ideologically minded Jewish European intellectuals and victims of the German and the Russian police states.

His autobiography—one sees clearly in this second volume, which is so much better than the first *(Arrow in the Blue)*—has a double mission: on the one hand, to depict the author as the typical representative voice from beyond the tomb; on the other, to assert his own identity. On the one hand, he is pure victim, product of the circumstances of his time in his intellectual development as much as in the kicks he has received from fortune; on the other, he has refused to be a martyr or a saint. His prayer when he was condemned to death, in 1937, in the Francoist prison cell at Malaga was that he might retain not the virtues of his suffering but the human faults which gave him an assurance of his own being: "Do not blackmail me, Lord God, and do not try to make a saint of me. Amen."

Considering Koestler thus as the type of resurrected victim from Central Europe—also typical in having had all the experience and invented for himself all the ideas of such a type—it may well be a major misfortune of our time that the good Lord granted his prayer so completely, singling him out as one who is decidedly not a saint. It would surely be reassuring to think that those who had represented communism were pure and just and virtuous. It is surely distressing to feel that they may have rejected communism partly on account of all the human characteristics which are still with them. Koestler leaves us with a suspicion that if he were a Communist for idealist reasons, he is an anti-Communist largely for the sake of being Koestler. This is the more so because phrases like the chapter heading, "The Crusader Without Cross," and titles like *Arrow in the Blue, The Invisible Writing,* etc., suggest a goal which has been attained; but when we look closer, there is a feeling of emptiness, as though we had been left with a phrase.

Perhaps such catchwords indicate a blank space in his development which Koestler will not be able to evade filling in. Meanwhile, adding up the whole sum of his autobiography, we should recognize that it is a very great achievement to have such a typical case history and to insist so violently on retaining an identity that tries his contemporaries to the point of exasperation.

Most of this volume describes Koestler as a Communist. It opens with an account of him as a secret party member, in 1932, working for two German liberal newspapers, and gaining information from bourgeois friends, which he passes on to his "cell." However, within that same year he abandons this role and goes to Russia, with the idea of writing a book rather hypocritically entitled: *Russia Through Bourgeois Eyes.* The weak link in the chain that bound Koestler to the comrades was his inability ever to write anything which pleased them. Book after book was submitted to the party critics and condemned as too individualistic.

Meanwhile he made enormous journeys through the Soviet Union, writing his propaganda which was unconsciously double-edged: "...Let us not deceive ourselves: this writer did not stand up very well to the test of the first few days. He splashed about rather helplessly in the bottomless porridge of impressions...," and so on. He traveled the length and breadth of the Soviet Union, convinced that he saw good wherever he went. Yet when he took up his pen he wrote down things which the artist in him had pierced through the ideological blinkers. He traveled to Mount Ararat, Baku, Turkestan and to the Afghan frontier: few journalists can have seen more of the Soviet Union at the stage of its development when the great purges were just beginning.

Like most great diarists and observers, Koestler seems to live his life for the purpose of writing down an interesting narrative. The historic background is relieved with romantic love affairs, much more vividly described than in the more cynical pages of *Arrow in the Blue*. The present volume excels in portraits of women he loved and friends he admired, like the Hungarian poet, Attila, and the neurotic hostess, Maria. There is also excellent light relief in his account of writing *The Encyclopedia of Sexual Knowledge*, published under the pseudonym, Dr. A. Costler.

Like many others, Koestler might well have become disillusioned with Russian communism, had it not been for the Reichstag Fire trial, and the Spanish Civil War, which diverted attention from the monstrous Moscow trials. The climax of this volume is the events in Spain, leading to his arrest by the Francoists and his imprisonment in a condemned cell. It was the experience of solitary confinement under sentence of death which enabled him to see through the ethics of communism, though he did not yet reject its political program:

> In the social equation, the value of a single life is nil; in the cosmic equation, it is infinite....Not only communism, but any political movement which implicitly relies on purely utilitarian ethics, must become a victim to the same fatal error. It is a fallacy as naive as a mathematical teaser, and yet its consequences lead straight to Goya's Disasters, to the reign of the gullotine, the torture-chambers of the Inquisition, or the cellars of the Lubianka.

It is difficult to give an idea of the immense range and variety of this book. Among other things I have not mentioned, there are meetings with Freud and Thomas Mann; and an account of Koestler's preparations for writing his novel *The Gladiators*, about Spartacus, which must fill every fellow-writer with sympathetic admiration. Koestler, to describe his characters, studied "such far-fetched subjects as the nature and shape of Roman underwear....I found it impossible to write a scene if I could not visualize how the characters were dressed, and how their garments were held together." Strange as it may seem, there are few passages here that convince me more of Koestler's seriousness.

In spite—and perhaps because—of his references to his many "complexes," the character of Koestler himself in his autobiography remains controversial and rather enigmatic. Certain obvious things do not seem to occur to him: for example that if one keeps on referring to one's "inferiority complex" it becomes a kind of asset and therefore must cease to be so inferior. The true nature of his inner struggle seems covered over by much analytic terminology. At heart Koestler seems to me a religious man in search of penitence, homesick for a communion of saints. And in spite of his courageous self-examination, he does not seem to have discovered that his basic fault is pride.

Looking Back on Koestler's Spanish War

by Murray A. Sperber

Of the extraordinary amount of literature that came out of the Spanish Civil War, Arthur Koestler's work is considered among the best, usually ranked with the personal narratives of Orwell and Bernanos and the fiction of Hemingway. In 1954, in his most specific comment on his Spanish War writings, Koestler explained:

> In all foreign editions, including the American, *Dialogue with Death* appeared as a self-contained book. In the original English edition, however (Gollancz and Left Book Club, 1937), it formed the second part of *Spanish Testament*, the first part of which consisted of the earlier propaganda book on Spain that I had written for Muenzenberg *(L'Espagne ensanglantée)*. *Spanish Testament* is (and shall remain) out of print; *Dialogue with Death* has been reissued in England under that title, in the form in which it was originally written.[1]

Most of Koestler's textual information is incorrect. He does not tell us that he has made crucial changes from text to text: the first half of *Spanish Testament* "consisted of" more — over a hundred pages more — than "the earlier propaganda book," *L'Espagne,* and the "Dialogue" section of *Spanish Testament* was significantly altered for *Dialogue with Death* — there are hundreds of major and minor deletions and additions. The revisions, in fact, point to important changes in Koestler's politics, personality, purposes, and literary skills.[2]

"Looking Back on Koestler's Spanish War," by Murray A. Sperber. From *The Dalhousie Review*, LVII (Spring, 1977). Reprinted by permission of the author.

[1]*The Invisible Writing: The Second Volume of an Autobiography,* 1932-1940, Hutchinson and Co., London, 1969, 411.

[2]The critics are no help in unravelling Koestler's Spanish writings; when they discuss *Dialogue with Death,* they assume that there is only one text and that it was written in 1937 — whereas the text they usually quote from is the greatly revised 1942 edition.

In their author's eyes, *L'Espagne* and *Spanish Testament* belong to an earlier period of his life: they were written while he was still in the Communist Party and before he had felt the full effect of his Spanish War experience. In shedding his past, he also obscures some of its artifacts. His motives, however, seem less malicious (he need not have mentioned the texts) and more the result of psychological suppression. Koestler's Spanish Civil War experience was so difficult—his visits to Spain under Comintern auspices, his capture by Franco's troops, the Spanish prison cells, his discovery of self, his subsequent break from the Communist Party, as well as his writings about Spain—that in his later statement, he prefers to see the whole writer who emerged at the end, rather than the man, often in chaos, who lived through it. Instead of regarding *L'Espagne* and *Spanish Testament* as his doors of perception and the record of his journey, he finds the recollection of them so painful that he is glad to report, they are "(and shall remain) out of print."

In fact, all of Koestler's versions of his Spanish Civil War experience are worth the light of print and together, they form a unique microcosm of a period—the most important literary period—of his life. In *L'Espagne,* essentially a Comintern propaganda book, replete with atrocity stories and horrifying photographs, he reveals his ambivalent and doomed infatuation with the Communist Party as well as his dependence upon Willy Muenzenberg, the Comintern's "Red Eminence" (Koestler's phrase). In the first half of *Spanish Testament,* on his own in England, he falls into various didactic styles: sometimes he is the echo of Comintern propaganda, often he quiets to passages of liberal reason, and frequently he turns Marxist analysis into apocalyptic vision. But in the second or "Dialogue with Death" half of the book, he allows his individualism to emerge. Then, in the separate *Dialogue with Death* edition of 1942, he drops the chapters of historical and political analysis, over 180 pages, and concentrates on his private adventures in Spain, especially in the prisons of Malaga and Seville. The three different but complementary texts form a kind of modern *Bildungsroman:* the hero's character emerges from the trials and temptations of politics to discover spiritual meaning and to be born anew. By disregarding the author's textual misinformation, therefore, and working through all of his Spanish War writings, we can read and evaluate them in a different, certainly a more accurate way.

L'Espagne ensanglantée (Editions du Carrefour, Paris, 1937) is written in a hectic, scattered, at times almost bloodthirsty style. Koestler worked under the direction of Willy Muenzenberg, head of the Comintern's Paris propaganda office, and his writing reflects Muenzenberg's literary injunction: "'Hit them! Hit them hard!... Make the world gasp with horror. Hammer it into their heads. Make them *wake up*...!'" (*Invisible Writing*, 407). To establish Koestler's credibility, an editorial note describes him as an *"Envoye special du News Chronicle, journal liberal de Londres"* (*L'Espagne*, 9). (Muenzenberg arranged this cover and throughout his trips to Spain, Koestler did send a number of dispatches to the *News Chronicle*.) In the opening chapters of *L'Espagne*, he tells of his journey into Rebel territory in August, 1936. He reports on Fascist atrocities in Seville (most of these accounts were dropped for *Spanish Testament* and therefore, were probably untrue), he visits the headquarters of the mad Rebel general, Queipo de Llano and quotes from the latter's famous radio broadcasts, e.g., *"Ces femmes communistes et anarchistes, par leur doctrine de l'amour libre, se sont elles-mêmes déclarés prêtes à appartenir au premier venu"* (*L'Espagne*, 23). He then leaves Spain.

His personal adventures are muted, and he focuses the narrative on the Nationalist campaign. He retails, at length, atrocity stories and he participates fully in the propaganda war of the time. Years later, he portrayed himself as almost innocent in the writing of *L'Espagne*, as if he were mainly Muenzenberg's amanuensis, but considering Koestler's talent for vivid prose, he was probably more than a passive copyist when the atrocity stories were ladled into the book.

Koestler never states his personal feelings in *L'Espagne* but he suggests his confusion and pessimism. He fears lying—and according to his later memoirs, he felt that his life in the Communist Party was mainly a lie—and he says of propagandists: *"Un agitateur qui connait son métier peut repandre dans le monde, en dix minutes, plus des mensonges que l'on en pourra réfuter au course d'une année"* (*L'Espagne*, 45). He is referring to Hitler and, indirectly, Goebbels and Franco, but since he and Muenzenberg were engaged in Comintern propaganda, he implies a self-description as well.

After finishing *L'Espagne*, possibly to break out of his psychological and, at times, financial, political, and literary dependence upon and frequent rejection by Willy Muenzenberg (Koestler had been with him on and off for four years), he embarked upon other missions to Spain. That his psychic situation was becoming intolerable and that he felt compelled to cut through it by an extreme and dangerous act is one explanation of why, on February 9, 1937, after rejecting numerous opportunities to leave the doomed city of Malaga, Koestler allowed himself to be captured by Rebel troops.

It was the London *News Chronicle,* ironically, after a vigorous campaign protesting the arrest and imprisonment of an "English liberal journalist," who helped most to secure his release from Nationalist Spain. He spent ninety days in prison, first in Malaga and then in Seville, under sentence of death and with no idea of what was occurring on the outside. Suddenly he was released, taken to Gibraltar and then to England, where he found himself front page news.

Immediately, for the *News Chronicle,* he wrote a factual, journalistic account of his adventure. In the five articles (May 23 to May 28, 1937), he described his arrest and imprisonment, including drawings of his cell, but he hardly mentioned his psychological experiences. The very last line of the final article indicates his feelings at this time: "It is still like a dream..." (his ellipsis).

Koestler's situation in England in late May, 1937, was complicated: if he revealed that he was a Communist, he would embarrass the people who had helped to secure his release and justify "Franco's propaganda which took the line that all democratic opponents of his regime were disguised Reds" (*Invisible Writing,* 448). He felt that he had to maintain "the fiction of the *bona fide* Liberal journalist" and "A deception, once started, has a compelling momentum of its own" *(ibid.).*[3] But possibly the role of liberal journalist was less troubling than continuing membership in the Communist Party. England, with its tradition of individualism, allowed Koestler's individualism to flower. During his political career on the Continent from 1931 to 1937, he had never squared his individualism with the

[3]In fact, the liberal British press and public were using Koestler as much as he claims to have used them. The press campaign sought to embarrass Franco and more directly, the non-interventionist Chamberlain government. The *News Chronicle* ran such headlines as, "Fears for Koestler: Tied to Plank in Cell" [an untrue rumor], April 7, 1937, and "Koestler: Union Jack was No Protection" [he was an Hungarian citizen], April 15, 1937.

demands of Party discipline—it was this struggle that shaped his off-again-on-again participation in the Party—but once in England, he could free himself of the major deception of his life—his self-deception concerning CP membership. In England, he could be rewarded financially, socially, and psychologically for working out in print what he termed his "voyage of discovery" (*Spanish Testament*, 301), and although under the restraint of having to pose as a liberal journalist, he found that less confining than Willy Muenzenberg's Comintern tutelage.

After completing his series for the *News Chronicle*, Koestler was asked by Gollancz to do a book on his Spanish adventures. When he wrote *Spanish Testament* in the summer and fall of 1937, his sense of self was very much in transition and the book reflects the transition.[4] In the first half of *Spanish Testament*, he unsuccessfully combines elements of the propagandist's contempt for his audience with the liberal journalist's sympathy for a like-minded, individualist reader. Only when he defines the line between himself and "English journalists in particular, with their traditional feelings for level-headedness and decency. ... But a civil war is in itself a somewhat indecent affair" (*Sp. T.* 164), does he move toward his own voice (and his eventual role as exile and prophet within English life and letters). So much for the public side of liberal journalism, Koestler is after the private element, subjective truth, and when he seeks it in the second half of *Spanish Testament*, "Dialogue with Death," the propagandist gives way to the psychological pilgrim and the author produces a coherent narrative.

Unlike *L'Espagne ensanglantée*, Koestler begins *Spanish Testament* with a first-person narrator and he tells the story of his initial visit to and escape from Rebel Spain (a Nazi journalist in Seville recognized him and he had to flee). He saturates the narrative with atrocity stories and luridly describes his adventures: during his interview with Queipo de Llano, "Spittle oozed from the corners of the General's mouth, and there was [a] flickering glow in his eyes

---

[4]Part of the transition was his increasing use of the English language in his writing. Stanley Weintraub in *The Last Great Cause*, Weybright and Talley, New York, 1968, states that "more than half of *Spanish Testament* (including *Dialogue with Death*) was originally written in English," and he offers as his source, "Koestler to S[tanley] W[eintraub], June 7, 1965" (p. 321).

..." (*Sp. T.* 34). After the opening narrative, he launches a "Historic Retrospect" section, five chapters, one hundred and eighty pages in all, much of it cribbed from *L'Espagne*. But the changes are significant: the argument has been smoothed out, charts put into words, and English references added. The entire first half of *Spanish Testament* suggests that Koestler had not resolved his confusion and ambivalence about Willy and the Party—he did not resign for another six months—but at the same time, he sought a way out of the tension that his past created.

One of his solutions, mainly unconscious, was to fasten upon the apocalyptic element in Marxism. In passages that could have roared from the author of *The Eighteenth Brumaire*, Koestler shows how he had internalized Marx's apocalyptic style. Frequently he calls for the total break from the past—"once and for all sweeping away the economic foundations of feudalism in Spain"—and he sees no easy or reformist way to "the new era"—history requires revolution and apocalypse and "The receipt for [Republican] tolerance was handed...by General Franco on July 18th, on the point of a bayonet" (*Sp. T.* 65).

He goes beyond Marxism, however, in his fascination for and portrayal of the apocalyptic. For the political role of the Catholic Church, he invokes the rich Medieval apocalyptic tradition: "Infuriated crowds made attacks on churches and monasteries; they had not forgotten that...the machine-guns of antichrist had been trained on them from the fortress-like sacred building of Spain" (*Sp. T.* 67). The Nationalist Rebellion becomes "that curious blend of poison gas and incense which is characteristic of Francisco Franco's modern crusade" (*Sp. T.* 60). And the Moorish troops are the agents of apocalypse, demonic hordes embarked on "the barbarians' crusade" (*Sp. T.* 71).

That the Spanish Civil War prompted these apocalyptic descriptions was as much a result of the actual historical situation as Koestler's personal need and desire to focus on this aspect of it. He was hardly alone in seeing the war as apocalyptic, but because he saw his life at this time as a series of catastrophes, he was attracted to the most catastrophic element in the Spanish War.

The apocalyptic mode, however, allowed him a way out of his personal dilemma. Too often in the first half of *Spanish Testament*, he loses control because he cannot construct a framework within which to resolve his political, psychological, and literary tensions. Instead he erects a centrifugal machine, throwing its elements from the center. Only when he connects his private fears to world destruction fantasies, describing personal experiences in apocalyptic terms, does he locate his authentic voice.

This occurs in the second half of the book, "Dialogue with Death." A key passage, identical in the 1937 and 1942 texts, describes his thoughts on the eve of the fall of Malaga, with an Italian Army outside the defenseless city.[5] He begins with a solemn incantation of the date, this important day in the life of Malaga (and of Arthur Koestler because of his arrest): "On this Sunday night, the seventh of February, nineteen hundred and thirty-seven, a new St. Bartholomew's Night is being openly prepared" (*Sp. T.* 210/*Dial.* 32). His biblical cadence and imagery turns "An army of foreign invaders... encamped beyond the hills, recouping its strength" into a demonic horde, and he builds on this when he announces that "to-morrow," they "will invade these streets and drench them in the blood of the people." He plays on the phrase, "the blood of the lamb," because the people are childlike and innocent and the invaders, characterized by the repeated "they," senselessly cruel: "whose [the people's] language they do not understand, with whom they have no quarrel, and of whose very existence they were yesterday as unaware as to-morrow they will be indifferent to their deaths" *(ibid.)*.

There is no indication of this passage in the *News Chronicle* series. Later in "Dialogue," Koestler describes the Nationalist take-over of Malaga—the town was almost deserted, it proceeded smoothly, with hardly a shot fired—and thus he acknowledges that his "St. Bartholomew's Night" did not occur. But six months after the fall of Malaga, he wrote this passage for "Dialogue" and four years later he kept it in *Dialogue*. The apocalyptic mode must have seemed absolutely true to him, representative of his feelings at the time, and as with most writers who invoke the apocalypse, he transmutes the political and psychological experience that sparked his feelings into annunciatory terrors. The final line of the passage— "There is still perhaps time to get away"—shows the connection be-

[5]For the reader's convenience, all *Dialogue with Death* references are to the inprint Macmillan paperback edition (it is identical to the 1942 Macmillan edition).

tween his demonic horde on the other side of the hills and his own person. Koestler, in fact, did not try to get away.

In "Dialogue"/*Dialogue,* Koestler tells the story of his imprisonment and his discovery of self. He later said that this was part of "the most important period in my life, its spiritual crisis and turning point" but "the transformation...took some time [to] seep through and alter my conscious outlook" (*Inv. Wr.* 411-412). The before-and-after Koestler exists particularly in the textual differences between "Dialogue" (1937) and *Dialogue* (1942).

In the Foreword to "Dialogue," Koestler refers to himself as "a writer" and "a journalist," but for the 1942 Foreword, he mentions "the first person singular" and his string of "I's" leads into the first-person narrative of the text (throughout *Spanish Testament,* he had moved fitfully from third to first person and back again).

The successive Forewords point to Koestler's emerging individualism, and every change in the text underlines his new sense of self, as author, subject, political man, and psychological phenomenon. In the first half of *Spanish Testament,* the liberal journalist alternated with the leftist ideologue; in the "Dialogue with Death" half, when he concentrates on his personal experiences, he begins to work out the authorial synthesis that he completes in *Dialogue:* the lone individual within an apocalyptic world. In his life, especially after he left the CP in 1938, he moved to increasing isolation, in his writing, to prophecy. (During these five years, he finished *The Gladiators,* and wrote *Darkness at Noon* and *Scum of the Earth* —three of his most powerful and prophetic books.)

The major differences between "Dialogue" and *Dialogue* are personal and literary. Again and again, he reworks a passage or changes a word or two to emphasize his authorial character and/or to produce a greater literary effect. No doubt he rewrote partly because of his increasing familiarity with the English language and his dissatisfaction with the original text, but in so doing he also indicates his growing sense of himself as a writer, even a literary artist.

He takes turgid "Dialogue" passages of hundreds of words and by eliminating the verbiage, and often the sloppy sentiments, turns them into vivid, concise paragraphs. When he adds to the text, he gives it greater rhetorical force. His narrative character is more carefully drawn and he is more honest about his emotions. As part of his description of his breakdown in Malaga on the eve of surrender, he adds the paragraph: "Nothing doing without alcohol. The pressure of outward events has to be balanced by a certain inward pressure; the brain remains lucid but stark reality is agreeably blunted. And one no longer minds" (*Dial.* 21).

On the formal literary level, the deletion or addition of words, Koestler seems quite conscious; but on the political and psychological levels—the meanings and implications of these changes—he appears much less aware. He can present some of his private feelings, as in the passage on alcohol, but he is still unable and/or unwilling to tell the whole story of his Spanish War experiences. *Dialogue* has a more polished surface than the earlier version but Koestler's unconscious projections still break through, usually in odd, code-like ways. In a passage added for *Dialogue,* he describes a zealous political commissar:

> He is twenty-five and has been a member of the Socialist Youth from the age of eighteen. He knows all about the situation, and he knows that I know all about it, and that to-morrow the entire world will know all about it even if I don't cable a word. But his grey matter, soaked with propaganda, is proof against all realization of the truth.
>
> (*Dial.* 27)

The biographical detail that the fellow has been in leftist party politics for seven years (the years 1930-1937) appears gratuitious until connected to Koestler's own years in the Party: "I served the Communist Party for seven years (1931-1938)."[6] He seems both to identify with the young Spanish politico and be repulsed by him. Since he added this to his text after he had ended his CP years, the "he," the politico, can be translated as the old, CP Koestler, and the "I" as the newly isolated and aware author writing about the "soaked with propaganda" politico.

Usually the *Dialogue* revisions are more in control than in this passage. Sometimes the changes are subtle and reflect an impulse to try to reenter and recreate feelings, especially those of his prison experience, and by implication, to reject the earlier version as in-

[6]*The God That Failed,* ed. Richard Crossman, Bantam Books, New York, 1965, 59.

complete or inaccurate. In 1937, in his conclusion to "Dialogue,"
he cannot articulate what has happened to him and as the "St. Barth-
olemew Night's" passage showed, he found it easier to project apocalyptic feelings upon Malaga, even Spain itself, than to focus on the
momentous changes in his own life:

> Still more often I dream that I must return to No. 41 [his Seville
> prison cell] because I have left something behind there. Something
> or other, I don't know what.
>   What was it, what have I forgotten? I must go back once again and
> take a last look round before the steel door falls to: this time not be-
> fore, but behind, me.   (*Sp. T.* 369)

When he comes to rewrite this passage for *Dialogue,* he has a better
sense of what has occurred:

> Still more often I dream that I must return to No. 41 because I have
> left something behind there. I think I know what this something is, but
> it would be too complicated to explain.   (*Dial.* 202)

"Dialogue"/*Dialogue* ends with Koestler flying out of Nationalist
Spain in a small, open plane. The movement of the plane and the
spectacular sensation of clouds, earth, and sky are reminiscent of
the final flight in Malraux's *Temps de Mépris* (there, too, the political prisoner is flown to his freedom amidst much overt symbolism).
For *Dialogue,* Koestler adds the Epilogue statement:

> Those who survived are now pursuing their dialogues with death in
> the midst of the European Apocalypse, to which Spain had been the
> prelude.   (*Dial.* 215)

Koestler later chose to bury the first half of *Spanish Testament*
and to deny the nature of the "Dialogue" half. Unfortunately for
Dialogue with Death, the first half of *Spanish Testament* supplies
a rhetorical element necessary for the whole *Dialogue* experience.
Although the historical background is often inaccurate and overstated, in *Spanish Testament,* unlike *Dialogue,* the main participant,
Arthur Koestler, is placed within history. Even when he tries to
objectively present the background, he is subjectively involved. He
is a partisan, and he convinces us, rightly, that there is no shame in
being on the side of the Spanish Republic.

Spanish Testament is also crucial to *Dialogue* because within the first half of the book, Koestler captures the apocalyptic climate of the Spanish Civil War. He portrays and participates in the level of feeling that can lead men to kill "Reds" or "Fascists," "Workers" or "Priests," simply because they can pin those labels on their victims. By conveying this passion in the first half of *Spanish Testament,* he helps explain how and why the Seville prison and its executions can operate in *Dialogue.* Without the passion of the first half of *Spanish Testament,* reading *Dialogue* is somewhat like coming in for the last act of a drama: the level of emotion seems inappropriate to what is happening on stage.

An example of this discrepancy occurs when he is arrested in Malaga:

> While we are crossing the forecourt an officer of the Phalanx [Falange] prodded me on the chest. "*Ruso, Ruso*—a Russian, a Russian!" he exclaimed in the excited voice of a child which, when taken to the zoo for the first time, shouts: "A crocodile, a crocodile!" I said that I was not a Russian, but he wouldn't listen to me.
>
> "Tonight you'll be flying off to your Moscow Hell," he said with a grin.   (*Sp. T.* 227/*Dial.* 52-53)

Within the context of *Spanish Testament,* after the long discussions of propaganda, especially the virulence and power of Franco's anti-Communist campaign, the Falangist's reaction makes sense. Without the context, as in *Dialogue,* his actions seem at once comic and gratuitously sadistic.

When, in the truncated version, Koestler begins his *Dialogue with Death,* he sees it personally, with few political implications. By leaving out the first half of *Spanish Testament* and rewriting the "Dialogue" half, his perceptions about death often become small, ironic jests. With a coherent *Spanish Testament,* all parts of *Dialogue* would assume a larger dimension: the relationship of politics to a man's life and death. *Dialogue* is merely that—a dialogue between a single man and the peculiar forces of his possible death (a sudden, almost unexplained potentiality). *Spanish Testament* might have been that—a testament to a wider experience.

Koestler has told the story of his Spanish War experiences one other time. In *Invisible Writing,* 1954, he attempted to analyse his motives and actions during his visits to Spain and describe his mystical experiences in cell No. 41. In five chapters, sixty-two pages in all, with great intensity, he tries to reenter and relive his Spanish War experience. The result is a form of therapeutic catharsis, one to complete as well as articulate what had occurred during the original experience. At one point in *Invisible Writing,* after connecting a troubling and recurring dream to a prison incident, he says, "the feeling of guilt on this particular count began to dissolve, and I began to take a more detached view of the incident" (439). The psychic relief that comes from telling his most private version of the experience also allows Koestler to see his writings on the war in a new way—but to the end, he confuses the "Dialogue" half of *Spanish Testament* with the *Dialogue* revision:

> *Dialogue with Death* is an autobiographical sketch written at the age of thirty-two; the present chapter is an "explanation" of the same events, written at the age of forty-seven. I wonder what shape and colour they would take if I were to re-write them after another fifteen years have elapsed. Yet in intent each of these versions represents the truth, based on first-hand knowledge of the events and intimate acquaintance with the hero   (*Inv. Wr.* 442)

He reveals his dialectical sense here; rather than try to arrest time as he so frequently did in the earlier versions, he acknowledges its flux and even seems content to flow with it.

Because of such moments, as well as the intensity that drives him through his self-examination, Koestler's Spanish War writings form a series of remarkable documents. When the 1954 memoir was published, some critics compared it to Rousseau's *Confessions.* Koestler's work is far too flawed to achieve Rousseau's rank but his Spanish War writings are important and when considered together, they form a unique record of a man's personal, political, and literary odyssey.

Writing was so integral to the experience that the works map the journey: from Communist Party propagandist and Willy Muenzenberg's agent in *L'Espagne ensanglantée,* through the *News Chronicle* and *Spanish Testament* contradiction of liberal journalist and leftist ideologue, to Arthur Koestler, individual hero and prophetic figure in "Dialogue with Death" and especially its revision, *Dialogue with Death,* and finally, the self-analyst and mystic of *The Invisible Writing.* In their contradictions, unevenness and brilliance, Koestler's Spanish War writings reaffirm Isaac Rosenfeld's judgment that "it is precisely his limitations, by which he reflects his age, that give his utterances their authenticity for the age."[7]

---

[7]Isaac Rosenfeld, "Palestinian Ice Age," *The New Republic,* November 4, 1946, 592.

PART TWO

Science and Mysticism

Arthur Koestler's *Insight and Outlook*

by James R. Newman

The subtitle of Arthur Koestler's latest work is "An Inquiry Into the Common Foundations of Science, Art and Social Ethics." It is also described as a "book on the psychology of the higher mental functions." The publisher tells us that Koestler spent five years "reading widely in the fields of biology, neurology and psychology" in preparing himself to "do for philosophy what Einstein attempted for physics in his 'unitary field theory,'" I am therefore somewhat appalled at the task of reducing this epic achievement to the humdrum prose of the reviewer; but if I am to say anything intelligible about what Koestler refers to as "our theory," there is no alternative but to be bold.

His jumping-off-place is a new theory of the comic. It is not, in truth, entirely new, as Koestler himself points out, since he borrows freely from Henri Bergson *(Le Rire),* Sigmund Freud *(Wit and Its Relation to the Unconscious)* and from a number of their predecessors. However, the special blend of literary-medical-philosophical-psychoanalytical-biological lingo and the mental-circuit diagrams in the book are more or less Koestler's own products; and the ambitious extension of conclusions derived from an analysis of humor to all other forms of mental behavior bears his very own mark.

Koestler starts his long journey to the heartland of insight with the aid of a number of stories quoted from Freud, Bergson and others. They serve to introduce his "discovery" that the "essence of the comic is the bisociation of two operative fields in a junctional concept which is a member of both."

The formidable terms used by Koestler are perhaps best illustrated by means of two stories:

(1) "M. DuPont, an elderly notary of Clermont-Ferrand, has for years suffered from the annoying habits of his clerk Jules. Returning home unexpectedly from a journey, he finds Jules in bed with his wife. M. DuPont surveys the scene with a mournful eye and says: 'That is enough, Jules! Once more and you are fired.'"

(2) "A dignitary of Monte Carlo is much admired for the not less than 36 medals which he wears on his breast. Somebody asks him by what heroic deeds he earned them. 'That's simple,' he says, 'I got a medal for my faithful service to the prince; I put it on a number at the roulette table and the number came up.'"

The "intellectual geometry" of these droll stories is, according to Koestler, quite simple. It consists in something like the diagrams [below] which mean something like this:

As the tale is told there are "two unrelated association trains" which suddenly collide with each other at a given point. Each train is perfectly "logical" (*i.e.*, has its "operative field") and under normal circumstances "the stream of consciousness would follow either one branch or the other, for the two belong to different systems or planes of mental organization." At the collision of these two trains, however,

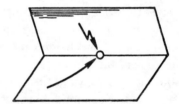

A JOKE is diagrammed by Koestler as intersection of fields. Listener laughs when narrative meets flash.

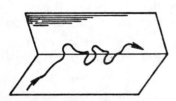

STREAM of consciousness wanders among fields. Reactions to stimuli depend on field tuned in at the time.

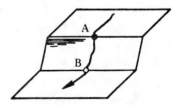

CHANGE in stream of consciousness requires a "junctional concept." In the diagram this is between A and B.

a new concept is born which "serves two masters at the same time....
it is *bisociated* with two independent and mutually exclusive fields."

As Koestler's blueprints plainly prove, at the point where the two
association trains collide, the joke (a new bisociated concept) flashes
into being and the auditor laughs. In M. DuPont's tale one thought
train relates to his business dealings with the unsatisfactory Jules, and
the other train to the familiar complex consisting in cuckold, wife,
paramour, and discovery *flagrante delictu.* The expectation of a
violent climax is suddenly "debunked" with a phrase from the em-
ployer-employee relationship.

Each train of a comic event may carry a different "emotional
charge" (*e.g.,* malicious, sexual, scatological), but it is the process
of combining habitually incompatible fields of thought that results
in the sudden release of tension and the explosion of laughter—
assuming, indeed, that there is laughter.

To explain how attention is focused on any one field, how the
mind is disciplined to concentration, Koestler proposes the concept
of the "selective operator." The operator defines its field in the
sense that it is a selective law, a "rule for manipulating ideas and
their verbal symbols." Operators may be simple and explicit, as in
a parlor game, for example, where the participants are to write down
within a time limit all the towns they can remember beginning with
the letter L. The class of all L towns—London, Lisbon, Lvov, etc.—
constitutes the operative field, and the L-rule is the selective operator. Operators may also be exceedingly complex and/or implicit,
just as the operative field may consist, among others, in a code, a
pattern of behavior, a chessboard and chessmen, a branch of mathematics, a musical or plastic art, a literary form.

Such is the technical apparatus used by Koestler in exploring
provinces other than the comic. Bisociation is the "characteristic
feature of any original creative process whether in art or in discovery," since every fresh synthesis entails the combination or union
of elements in previously separate areas of thought. Even the diagrams divised to exhibit the mechanics of the comic are, according
to Koestler, applicable to the processes of higher creativeness. The
separate fields joined in the creative synthesis are represented by
"planes," and the little straggling arrows represent separate trains
of thought association.

As for the concept of "emotive charge," it, too, like the "intellectual geometry" of the comic, has validity and significance in other spheres. In a humorous context the "common denominator" of the charge is "usually a very faint impulse of aggression or defense manifested as malice, derision, self-assertion, or merely as an absence of sympathy with the victim of the joke—a 'momentary anesthesia of the heart,' as Bergson puts it."

"The passion of laughter," said the English philosopher Thomas Hobbes, "is nothing else but sudden glory arising from a sudden conception of some eminency in ourselves, by comparison with the infirmity of others, or with our own formerly." From this starting point, Koestler develops the argument that the production of comic and certain other effects depends upon the dominance of this aggressive component or "self-assertive" tendency over the opposite tendency of "sympathetic identification" or "self-transcendence."

The integrative or self-transcending tendency, manifested with a certain simple purity in grief, is, in every human activity, in conflict with that of self-assertion. Every true act of creation, in whatever field, requires an expansion of the "range of awareness beyond the limits of self, or, conversely, of being aware of the self as part of a higher functional whole." The work of art, the generous impulse, the scientific discovery; the feeling of tenderness and protectiveness, the longing for martyrdom; the processes of "identification," "projection," "introjection," "transference," "sympathy" and "empathy"; the "oceanic" feeling, the mysticism and the wisdom of the East, the striving of the spike-sitting Hindu and the Hollywood Hindu toward "non-attachment"; the struggle to achieve, to improve and to extend social wholes—each of these, says Koestler, is evidence of the self-transcending urge.

What are the biological foundations of these tendencies? Koestler rests his interpretation on the "twin phenomena of differentiation and integration, which under conditions of stress become polarized into the conflicting tendencies of self-assertive and integrative behavior." A corollary function, of almost equal importance, is that of "regenerative equilibrium": an organism unable to cope with its environmental problems, or the conflict between its opposing tendencies, regresses to a lower biological, social or psychological level in order to start afresh by way of *"reculer pour mieux sauter"* (to retreat so as to get a better start for the jump).

Organized social wholes, Koestler contends, follow this biological pattern, not "morphologically," to be sure, but "functionally." Social organizations simply evince the integrative tendency on a higher level, though it is essential to realize that in the social field contemporary organizations correspond to fairly primitive organizations in the biological field. Sociologically we must be closer to the grub, say, than to anything quite so elaborate as a donkey.

Social wholes tend to grow weaker as they are isolated, as they grow too big and become unwieldy, as separate parts strive for autonomy, as communications are obstructed. Each of these circumstances contributes to self-assertiveness at the expense of the integrative self-transcending power. Within any given society, among individuals at different age levels, there are further illustrations of bipolarity and conflict. In the process of "maturation" a child's sense of oneness with the environment wanes and the self-assertive tendencies increase. In Western societies of course these tendencies are encouraged by the sacred slogans of competition and so on.

This, in Koestler's opinion, suffices to explain the crisis in present civilization. It is not, as Freud supposed, the suppression of man's destructive or death instinct that ails us. It is rather that we witness the "atrophy of the integrative tendencies in the social whole." Civilization is in the condition of a neurotic patient. To put civilization on a couch is difficult, and one may doubt that there is a therapist qualified to tackle the job of reintegration. (One may, I assume, dispense with any reference to the succor which might come from a supernatural power.)

Koestler pronounces the crisis "profound" and asserts that it must remain so until at least two conditions are fulfilled: "The final integration of national states into a global whole, and the adaptation of social organization to changes in the natural environment, that is, to the level reached in the technique of the exploitation of natural resources." But just as the neurotic may not survive a succession of crises because he is too sick to begin with, is unable to adjust his already unbalanced nervous pattern to fresh circumstances, or because the demands upon him may be too numerous and vehement, so it is unlikely, Koestler thinks, that western European civilization "has a sufficient regenerative span to survive until it attains this aim." Exactly where this leaves us is not clear.

So much for what, despite its length, is an extremely sketchy recapitulation of Koestler's large work. It would have been a good deal easier, I am convinced, to summarize in the same space Kant's *Critique,* Lotze's *Microcosmos,* or the writings of Arnold Toynbee. Apparently the seriousness of the subject and Koestler's conviction that this represents his *magnum opus* interfered with his well-known verbal dexterity. The result is something to behold. As he himself frankly admits, in trying to "strike a precarious balance between the claims of the general reader and of the specialist" he achieved a work in which "verbose passages boring to the scholar alternate with others over which the general reader may stumble." Not only is the writing afflicted with jargon and painful technical coagulations, but it is also evident that for fear of being thought an amateur in these many disciplines, Koestler wrote as only an amateur saddled with such a fear would write.

He is invariably long-winded and turgid, often unprecise and superficial. For example:

> The manifold fields or schemata of mental operations are selective matrices of acquired habits. They are, needless to say, not linear claims of conditioned reflexes but integrated habit patterns of extreme plasticity and adaptability. ... The concomitant increase of imaginative inertia and "clumsification" deprives the emotive of its lithe adaptability and supplies the sneer at unorthodox forms of art. ... Art is surprise in permanence. ... Benvenuto Cellini's golden saltcellar for Francis I is a source of aesthetic pleasure as well as a receptacle for salt. For—and this is the essential point—as it only functions as a receptable of salt for a few seconds during a long meal, what is it doing the rest of the time?

This latter question has baffled me for some years, but I regret to report that Koestler, having posed it, fails to give an answer.

What is new and original in these many pages? Koestler's theory of the comic, to which half the book is devoted, is largely a contrivance of borrowed parts with a new panache. The concepts of operative fields, selective operators, junctions and so on, contain no real innovations. "Bisociation," for all of Koestler's exertions to pass it off as a profound and revolutionary concept, proposes nothing essentially new. Koestler's theories of biology, especially of brain function, are naive restatements of certain current views; as a psychologist he adopts the "holistic, or organismic or Gestalt approach," with a few homemade embroideries. He strives to emphasize the difference between his theories of frustration, neuroses and social ills and those of Freud. He avers that his own theories are sustained by "overwhelming" biological evidence; but what he adduces by way· of proof is certainly less than overwhelming, though from my standpoint Freud's reductive simplifications are equally unsubstantiated. In short, Koestler advances old ideas, buttressed by current scientific hypotheses, many of the most speculative kind, the whole loosely bound together in a vague, grandiose, metaphor-ridden *Welt Philosophie* which smells a little of Hegel, Spengler and Freud.

Where Koestler conveys a first impression of originality is in his exposition of scientific ideas by the use of beguiling metaphors and enticing analogies. He senses the dangers inherent in this method of proof and warns of them; but the ingenious teller of tales triumphs over the amateur philosopher and scientist "Similitudes," said Thomas Fuller, "are the windows which give the best light," but the light of Koestler's similitudes is too often deceptive. The humor diagrams are inoffensive so long as it is clear that their purpose is only to show abstract relationships of abstract classes of ideas. Before long, however, one is led to believe that the separate planes of the diagrams have their physical counterparts in the brain, that each wiggling arrow is a wiggling motion in the brain cells. The very term "cognitive geometry" is ridiculously misleading if only in its implication that mental behavior is expressible in precise mathematical language. Koestler's description is complicated by the fact that at various times he likens the brain to a radio receiver, a tuning fork, a high-tension generator, a reservoir, a piano, a smooth pond, or a pond with ripples. It may be, I suppose, that the inside of the head corresponds to any or all of these objects, or it may, as in C. S. Sherrington's famous image, resemble a "great ravelled knot" twinkling with the tiny lights of thought and emotion. Yet until the matter has been settled I continue to feel uneasy, for it seems to me I have the right to know when deciding whether or not to subscribe to Koestler's theory how my head measures up to a Steinway, a Philco or a Westinghouse quarter-horsepower motor.

Koestler's extension of the self-assertive and self-transcending tendencies to the "inorganic level" leads to other strange conclusions.

Thus, "energy concentrations," as in elementary particles, and "the formation of molecules, crystals, and so on" are not merely examples of "structurally differentiated integrated [*sic*] patterns," but are "genetic precursors" of the two main behavior drives. And, "inertia, centrifugal momentum, free valences and so on" are in the same class as a malicious witticism in evincing "autonomous or self-assertive tendencies." It would be equally convincing and equally portentous—having first asserted that all things either gather or disperse, rise or fall, are positively or negatively charged, male or female, hot or cold—to deduce the nature of the world from any of these antitheses. In Koestler's dream all animals, vegetables, minerals and ideas are kin either to Francis of Assisi or to the practical joker. He says: "The first schoolboy to have the revolutionary idea of sawing through the legs of the teacher's chair was obviously a creative genius. His usual methods of satisfying aggressive impulses against other schoolboys...being inapplicable in the teacher's case, the operative fields of habit are blocked, and a creative stress results."

It is in Koestler's analysis of "discovery," *i.e.,* the "Eureka process," that his theory attains full flowering and its ripest absurdity. "Eureka!" it will be recalled, was Archimedes' cry as he ran naked through the streets of Syracuse, having just discovered, while taking his bath, how to determine whether there was an admixture of silver in the allegedly pure gold crown given to Hiero, the Tyrant, by his jewelers. The discovery was that of the hydrostatic law which states that the amount of weight lost by a body when immersed in water is equal to the weight of the water displaced. Koestler's version of "Archimedes' reasoning," which makes the greatest scientist of antiquity appear to be something of a half-wit, includes a diagram to show the condition of Archimedes' mind *before* the famous bath. It is shown in the top diagram [p. 131].

Koestler explains that Archimedes for some time failed to connect "the sensuous and trivial associative contexts of taking a hot bath with the scholarly pursuit of the measurement of solids." But at last he managed, by self-transcendence, to rise above the sensations of "heat and cold, fatigue and relaxation, sex and beauty and so on," and by a supreme effort wrenched his mind into a cusplike condition, portrayed in the bottom diagram.

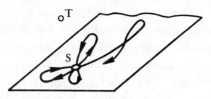

THOUGHTS of Archimedes before his
great discovery are schematized thus.
S represents the starting point.

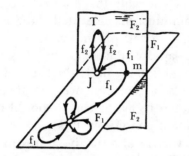

AFTER DISCOVERY Archimedes' mental
processes followed this path. At point T he
exclaimed, "Eureka!"

Koestler, apparently having been there while the thing was taking place, tells us finally that the exact moment of the great discovery was when "Archimedes saw his familiar hairy body as 'a solid which displaces a given amount of water.'"

The main flaw of the book, apart from its occasional sweeps of nonsense, its pretentiousness, pseudo profundity and non-stop quality, is its sterility. For all its bulk it says very little, because Koestler has very little to say. It lacks a real, driving principle or insight which could lead to fruitful conclusions. Despite Koestler's repeated denial that he advocates a simple dualism of nature, he seeks in fact to describe all events and substances, organic and inorganic, by a tautologous formula of "A or non-A." Nowhere is there a satisfactory explanation, in primitive terms, of the cause of either of his "tendencies" or of the mode of their evolution. His essay is studded with generalities about the nature of "cognition" but nothing concrete is said about how we come to know what we think we know. The attempts to formulate a serious, comprehensive theory of knowledge—essential to any such ambitious effort—are of the most jejune kind. Indeed, while Koestler pretends to a deep penetration of the classic problems of philosophy, he fails in fact to address himself to any of them. It never seems to occur to Koestler that a balanced, thorough examination of any mental state requires what one might call "algebraic" more than "geometric" reasoning. Such abstract factors as order, probability, inference, transformation, among others, are of course at the root of thought processes. Koestler mentions none of them. And as for social and political circumstances, it is amusing to note that by his own standards Koestler, the reformed Communist, has elevated the Soviet Union—insofar as it practices Marxism and pursues a rigidly planned economy— to a position at the apex of the hierarchy of "social wholes." For in Russia, where the rights of the individual are subsumed to the needs of all the toilers, "self-transcendence," in theory at least, would seem to have attained its apotheosis. I should not have thought it was the author's intention to prove this.

You may find a variety of attractive wares in Koestler's literary, philosophic, scientific and artistic delicatessen, but if you are shopping for insight and outlook, I suggest you go elsewhere.

Mr. Koestler's New System

by A. J. Ayer

Mr. Koestler describes his book, in a sub-title, as "an inquiry into the common foundations of science, art and social ethics." Many people may doubt whether any such common foundations exist, but Mr. Koestler believes that he has discovered them, and he has gone to considerable labour to show us what he thinks they are. He begins with a theory of the comic. In his view, we are stimulated to laugh when a train of thought, which is following a familiar associative track, is brought into contact with another train of thought which is not habitually associated with the first. The emotions which were attending the first train of thought are unable to make the jump, and so discharge themselves in laughter. These trains of thought need not be explicit; it is characteristic of many of the best jokes that the second train of thought is not fully elaborated, and the point of connection only hinted at. The emotions which are discharged in laughter may be of various kinds, but it is essential that they should be aggressive in character, or, as Mr. Koestler prefers to put it, self-assertive; and this aggressive element must be present from the start.

Now it is surely not the case that whenever anybody laughs at something he has been previously conscious of some self-assertive feeling; nor do I suppose that Mr. Koestler would wish to claim that it was. He would say, presumably, that these feelings were present unconsciously; but this is not very helpful if the only evidence for their unconscious existence is the fact that the person subsequently laughs. Unless there is evidence for their existence independently of the laughter they do not constitute an explanation of it. To this, if I understand him rightly, Mr. Koestler would reply that there was independent evidence, of a physiological character;

"Mr. Koestler's New System," by A. J. Ayer. From *The New Statesman and Nation,* XXXVIII (July 30, 1949), 127-128. Reprinted by permission of The New Statesman and Nation Publishing Company Ltd.

but although he writes at some length about the physiological con-
comitants of such self-assertive emotions as rage and fear, he does
not offer any proof that the same mechanisms operate in all cases
where a person is disposed to laugh. I do not wish to maintain,
however, that such a proof could not be given; and of course, if it
were it would very much strengthen Mr. Koestler's case.

The separate trains of thought whose junction provides the stimulus to laughter are said by Mr. Koestler to belong to different
"operative fields," and an idea which is associated with two operative fields is said to be "bisociated" with them. This concept of an
operative field is fundamental to Mr. Koestler's system, and it is
therefore unfortunate that it is never made at all precise. To begin
with, we are told that operative fields are "self-consistent and homo-
geneous systems" of "mental processes acquired by habit," each
system being subject to "a selective rule or structural law" which is
to be known as "the selective operator of the field"; but in the course
of the book the concept becomes so far extended that there is almost
nothing that it is not made to cover. Thus form and function, part
and whole, percepts and concepts, facts and laws, the trivial and the
tragic, illusion and reality are all treated as subjects for bisociation,
and so as pairs of operative fields. There is some suggestion even
that they form a hierarchy with the field of the oceanic feeling, over-
lapping with Jung's archetypal experiences, at the top. Now these
are important distinctions in their various ways, and Mr. Koestler
has many interesting things to say about them, but I cannot see that
much is to be gained by lumping them all together under one heading; and it can hardly be maintained that the terms enumerated
constitute, or even correspond to, opposing systems of habitually
associated ideas. If there is an habitual association, it obtains not
within these so-called operative fields, but between them. Whether
this is an objection to their being said to be "bisociated" is not clear,
for the term "bisociation" is used so widely that the consideration
of anything under different aspects, or from different points of view,
can apparently be counted as a bisociative process. Thus, to say of
something that it is yet another case of bisociation is to say very
little. We still require to analyse the particular relationships involved in each instance. To do him justice, Mr. Koestler frequently
undertakes such analyses and, in the case of aesthetic problems at
least, with considerable skill.

To the self-assertive emotions, which discharge themselves in laughter, Mr. Koestler opposes the self-transcending emotions which, when they are "redundant or frustrated" may be discharged in tears. These self-transcendihg emotions are held to be present in an enormously wide range of situations. What is common to them all is the absence of any sharply felt distinction between self and not-self. Thus, one asserts oneself against other people, but sympathises with them. Self-transcendence is not, however, confined to human relationships. It also takes place, for example, in all cases where a person is aware of himself as "part of a higher functional whole," in aesthetic contemplation, and, what will surprise philosophers, even in visual and acoustic perception, which is described as "a genuine perceptual symbiosis of the ego and its environment," on the ground that processes in the retina and within the ear are projected into space. An important difference which is supposed to obtain between the self-assertive and the self-transcending emotions is that the self-transcending emotions are able to follow thought in its movement from one operative field to another. Mr. Koestler makes considerable use of this property of the self-transcending emotions in his analysis of tragedy, and indeed of art in general, his conclusion being that "the aesthetic experience consists in the satisfaction of self-transcending impulses in internal behaviour."

Mr. Koestler finds a parallel between his two types of emotion and the separatist and integrative tendencies of the parts of certain organisms; and he draws what seems to me an even more dubious analogy between the functioning of animal organisms and that of political societies. His political recipe is greater integration, by which he seems to mean the self-surrender of the individual to the society conceived as an organic whole. This might perhaps pass as a description of what is likely to happen, but it is odd to find it submitted by Mr. Koestler as an ethical ideal. Of course he does not approve of totalitarianism as we now understand it. He says of the totalitarian states that they are faulty integrations. But if degree of integration is to be the only criterion, their faultiness must consist in their being excessively anarchic; whereas it appears to many of us that the fault is rather that they are not anarchic enough. So far as I can see, the reason why Mr. Koestler plumps for integration is that he identifies it with the self-transcending instincts and emotions;

and his fundamental ethical principle is that these are to be fostered at the expense of the self-assertive. This seems unexceptionable if it is construed as an appeal for the brotherhood of man; and no doubt this is what Mr. Koestler chiefly has in mind. I am sorry only that he found it necessary to link it with an organismic theory of society.

Turning to scientific discovery, Mr. Koestler brings it into the fold by describing it as a bisociative process with neutral emotional charge. The scientist's "exploratory drive" is emotionally neutral in the sense that it is a blend of the self-assertive and the self-transcending. "It can always be analysed into a component of competition or ambition, derived from the self-assertive tendency, and a second component of self-transcending absorption in the 'wonders' or 'mysteries' of nature." Having scientists for colleagues, I confess that I am sceptical about this second component. It would be more convincing and would suit Mr. Koestler's argument just as well, if he had merely ascribed to scientists a disinterested love of truth. The moment of thought which culminates in the decisive "bisociation" is described as the Eureka process, in memory of Archimedes. The defect of this example is that it is untypically dramatic; but it serves to bring out the point that scientific discoveries may establish connections between phenomena which had not so far been recognised. To say this, however, is not to say very much. An important fact, surely, is that scientific discoveries are usually made in the light of previous theories; and the expansion or modification of a theory may take very divergent forms. I doubt if it can always be represented as the junction of two operative fields; but this is a question that it is hardly profitable to argue until the notion of an operative field is made more precise.

Considering the book as a whole, I find that Mr. Koestler overworks his basic concepts. They come to mean too little because they are made to do too much. He is at his best when he turns aside from the larger generalities to argue particular questions of psychology or aesthetics. It should, however, be remarked that he has attempted no more in this book than to present a general outline of his system. A second volume is promised which will go into greater technical detail; and it is largely on the contents of this second volume that the scientific value of the system will have to be assessed.

Science and the Higher Truth

by *Stuart Hampshire*

Standards of knowledge and of rational understanding have been no less variable, no less in need of historical explanation, than the standards of beauty or of virtue. Why did men who had the necessary evidence for so long fail to draw the conclusions, to accept the explanation, which now seems to us obvious and unavoidable? Why did they cling to forms of explanation which now seem, judged by our standards, not to have been explanations at all? These are some of Mr Koestler's questions.[1]

In every age there is some preferred example of adequate knowledge and of clear understanding which serves as a model. Any new claim to knowledge, derived from sources that have never been used before, is always tested for legitimacy by a comparison with this prevailing model. An effort of imagination is always needed to understand the dominance of a now discredited ideal of natural explanation. Mr Koestler's history of cosmology reconstructs, with the added emphasis that is characteristic of him, the moments of breakdown and break-through, the first visionary steps towards a new pattern of natural knowledge and the anxious clinging to the old. The book is never for a moment dull. The author enters the drama himself, eagerly taking sides.

Our contemporary image of natural knowledge, pure and undefiled, is a mathematical physicist, scribbling a few equations which will explain the motions of everything everywhere and unlock "the secrets of matter." So dominating is this image that the word "science" is now apt to be used as if all science, as near as makes no difference, was simply mathematical physics. This happens

"Science and the Higher Truth," by Stuart Hampshire. From *The New Statesman and Nation*, LVII (January 31, 1959), 159-60. Reprinted by permission of The New Statesman and Nation Publishing Company Ltd.

[1][In *The Sleepwalkers: A History of Man's Changing Vision of the Universe* (London: Hutchinson & Co., 1959). — Ed.].

particularly when Science is pitted against Religion in one of those unreal public contests, during which their claims to final truth are compared. In an epilogue, and at intervals in his narrative, Mr Koestler compels those tired old war-horses, science and faith, to show their paces once again; and here again science seems to be simply identified with theoretical physics, as if all the sciences arrived at conclusions of the same form. Relying on that masterpiece of foreshortened history, Whitehead's *Science and the Modern World,* Mr Koestler thinks that contemporary consciousness is split. On one side there is "desiccated" scientific knowledge, on the other a now starved and separated faith in the spiritual destiny of men. The interest of his book seems to me to lie in the superbly sustained narrative, which extends from the Ionian philosophers to Newton, and in the vivid portraits of Tycho Brahe, Copernicus, and Kepler. But the philosophical thesis is aggressively there, important to the author, and cannot be left unquestioned.

Before the thesis could be accepted, I think that one would need to answer "Yes" to each of the following questions. First, on a matter of historical fact: was there a comfortable agreement on the limits of Christian faith and of free inquiry before the Renaissance destroyed it? Surely not: there was a running debate throughout the Middle Ages, to which Mr Koestler himself alludes. This debate continued, in changing forms, in the following centuries and will continue indefinitely, as long as there is rational theology. Secondly, is scientific inquiry necessarily, or even generally, "desiccating" and abstract? Again, No: delight in the discovered variety of nature, and in its complexities, may have been as much part of the inquirer's enjoyment as delight in the uniformity and simplicity of physical laws. The catalogue of nature is inexhaustible, and it is a reasonable guess that most scientists at any one moment have been engaged in bringing to light and naming new things and new forms. Nor is it true that colour, sounds and other qualitative differences must be disregarded in any genuine scientific inquiry. Thirdly, is it true that "the very framework of space and time turned out [*sc.,* in modern physics] to be as illusory as the taste, odours and colours which Galileo treated so contemptuously"? No: this was a disputed, and now generally rejected, philosophical interpretation of modern physics, and not a conclusion of physics itself. Fourthly, has there been a "progressive spiritual desiccation in post-Renaissance centuries"? No: this vague remark sounds like claptrap. Planck and Einstein, Sherrington and Fermi, do not seem to have been any more "spiritually desiccated" than any typical medieval thinker; and there is no evidence that study of the rational constructions of modern science has been found less inspiring, and less exciting, than study of the systems of the schoolmen. Lastly, is it possible to regard religion or faith as a single human interest, the loss of which is to be regretted? No: a religious man is not a man who believes in religion, but rather in a specific theology and in the rightness of a particular way of living which is founded upon it. It is arrogant, insulting almost, to wish that men were more religious, unless one believes that a certain religion is true. Mr Koestler is no doubt right in supposing that, in general and in the long run, the habit of scientific inquiry has tended to undermine the habit of Christian faith. Taken by itself, this fact is not to be regretted, as if religion was a matter of psychological health, a remedy for spiritual dryness. The question is: Have they been led away from the truth?

The fact that the range of ascertained truth about the natural order has become too various, and too intricate, for any one man to grasp, constitutes the real difference between the present and that earlier age of faith, which Mr Koestler regrets. This is the great disappointment of the system-builders. It has in effect changed the idea of natural knowledge, which in the seventeenth century was still thought easily exhaustible, when once the guiding principles had been found. This faith in the easy intelligibility of nature has gone. But its loss, like the corresponding loss of easy intelligibility in the arts, is much too simply described as a split in human consciousness.

However much one may disagree with Mr Koestler's philosophy, he is irresistible in his descriptions of the lives and characters of Tycho Brahe, Copernicus, and above all, of Kepler. Mr Koestler evidently likes this ill-favoured, generous, mystical, whimsical, garrulous genius, partly, perhaps, because he was so unlike a logical positivist. He was the most sleepwalking of the sleepwalkers. Guided by weird intuitions and an extravagant neo-Platonist philosophy, he walked, unsteadily and unaware, towards a devastating truth. But after six brilliant chapters at the centre of the book one enters that wasps' nest of controversy, the case of Galileo and the Church, and Mr Koestler becomes unpredictable, amazing.

As the author of some unfounded statements about Galileo's trial, based on discredited sources, I think I can recognise other unfounded statements, similarly based on ignorance, or at least the more obvious ones. They do not occur here. Mr Koestler has of course thoroughly considered the authorities, including Mr de Santillana's much discussed book, *The Crime of Galileo*. It is the bias in the commentary, and the tendency in the arrangement of the story, which are so odd and disquieting. Galileo had died eight years after he had been compelled by the Inquisition to deny, as a mere absurdity, his belief that the earth goes round the sun: the Pope had prohibited his friends from erecting a monument to the man who "had altogether given rise to the greatest scandal throughout Christendon." Summing up the case of Galileo, Mr Koestler's last sentence contains these words: "That was the end of one of the most disastrous episodes in the history of ideas: for it was Galileo's ill-conceived crusade which had discredited the heliocentric system and precipitated the divorce of science from faith." Discredited with whom and for how long? And who was finally discredited? The heliocentric system or the authorities of the Church? A little earlier one reads: "The only real penalty on Galileo was that he had to abjure his conviction." This of a passionate and proud man, old and ill and humiliated, who had been compelled to destroy part of his life's work, and who was, as Mr Koestler remarks, a "broken man" after his recantation: he returned from the ordeal to the Tuscan Embassy in Rome "more dead than alive." Mr Koestler graciously states that he does not "feel at liberty to criticise the change in his behaviour [*sc.*, his final and self-immolating recantation] before the Inquisition. He was seventy and he was afraid. That his fears were exaggerated...is beside the point." In the story that leads up to the humiliation, Galileo is presented as a would-be "superman" impelled by vanity: he was "beyond listening to reason" in teaching the superiority of the Copernican to the Ptolemaic hypothesis. It is suggested that he refused to accept the Church's offer of a compromise, and insisted on the physical truth of the hypothesis, partly because he could not yet produce any proof of it. After all, Mr Koestler cleverly argues, the new telescope by itself provided no proof:

the new observations could be made compatible with Tycho Brahe's system. This is of course true and, as special pleading, magnificent. The fact remains that Galileo was convinced of the physical truth of the hypothesis, having realised that the new observations made good sense, as physical realities, only when taken together with the new dynamics. Overestimating his influence with the authorities in the Church, and underestimating the ruthlessness of the reactionaries within the Church, and of his enemies outside, he thought that he could prevent the Church from coming down on the losing side of stupidity and error. But he failed and the scandal of his trial remains.

How horribly familiar it is, this ever present, anxious shuffle of the fellow-traveller, taking the long view, and preferring the Higher Truth. We have heard it all again recently. "If only he (Galileo or Pasternak) had waited a little longer..." "Why could he (Galileo or Pasternak) not have kept quiet and only expressed half the truth of his vision...?" "If only he had realised their difficulties..." "There were reasonable men among them..." "Things were just getting better..." Add another prong to the argument: show that the proponent of a new vision is vain, impetuous, excited, not a sensible man ready for compromise. Those who have new visions usually are uncompromising and obsessed, and particularly when presenting their life's work to the world in their old age. Mr Koestler's synthesis of science and faith is not likely to be a reliable friend of untimely truth, freely discovered and freely communicated. Rather it seems to be another name for Historical Necessity or the Higher Truth, that old friend waiting in the background.

There are five hundred pages of bold exposition of theories, with brilliant phrases, embarrassing phrases, philosophical reflections, laments about the modern world. All of it is intensely readable.

A Full-Blown Lily

by *William Empson*

It has immense impact; the arrival at Bombay which starts the
book must be the most gripping space landing in science fiction;
and the chapter "Yoga Unexpurgated" is far too horrible for me to
read. In between comes an account of "Four Contemporary Saints,"
and one is bound to feel the splendid breadth with which Hinduism
is being scrutinised, novelistically, mystically, scientifically, at
every level and through every chink. It's a rash fakir that looks gruff
at Koestler, let alone makes him stand in a queue; a sharp test of
sanctity there's going to be for that revered pagan, in the next batch
of press cuttings for him or her. The spirituality of the East and the
materialism of the West, one should readily agree, have become
harmful clichés which deserve attack; indeed the book would be
justified if the chapter on Yoga Research induced even one young
Indian on the verge of those practices to believe that their promise
of magical power is false. Even so, it is hard to believe that Indians,
owing to their neurotic fear of sex, are peculiarly unable to eat
curry.

The chief moral of the book is that Koestler is now proud to be a
Western European, as he is disillusioned with Zen and Yoga. But
India and Hinduism are not all Yoga, nor Buddhism and Japan all
Zen. After his renunciation of politics, one is interested to know
what he will recommend. He is indignant because Nehru planned
a Pink Utopia, suited to the Fabianism of the Twenties, or perhaps
because the Indians were too father-ridden to stop him. We are
given no reason to think that Nehru's plans were mistaken, and to
call them pink feels to me suited to Mosleyites in 1939. He conveys
powerfully the horror of the over-population of India, and then we

"A Full-Blown Lily," by William Empson, a review of Koestler's *The Lotus and
the Robot*. From *The New Statesman and Nation*, LXI (October 27, 1961), 21-22.
Reprinted by permission of The New Statesman and Nation Publishing Company
Ltd.

find him "depressed" because the Japanese have halved their birth-rate, or perhaps because they have legalised abortion. The book keeps on implying that he is less materialist than the Asians are, whereas it ought to be exposing the bogusness of that term.

In Japan the main thing he attacks is a certain silliness, already well known from previous tourists, and one might fear that this would be an anti-climax after the monstrosities of Ancient Night. But no, he manages to get the real Sunday-newspaper panting hor-ror into his description of the deportment of the young ladies; they are wired within, like the flowers. It is eked out with claims to intense sensibility: "I have lived through the London blitz and was bombed out by a V2, but this quite insignificant tremor is some-thing different." He has rather bad luck ("I felt, for instance, a curious affinity...") in his explanation of how footling the Noh plays are: "All violent emotions, like uncouth nature, have become... daintified." If he had waited to the end of the play, which only takes about an hour and a half, he would probably have found the ghost of the warrior doing a good old South Sea Island war dance, stamp-ing like a buck rabbit, to a terrific chorus of yowling. The forces of the world are strong at the climax in the music and dance, as they need to be since loyalty to them keeps the ghost from his peace; but, as they are not in the words, we tend to assume that the whole performance is just Celtic Twilight. Koestler would have had to blame the play for something different if he had sat it through. (By the way, I can't believe that Japanese madmen are never violent.) As to Zen, a mystical school which denies the value of explanation would be inconsistent if it gave a reporter sensible answers; but much of Japanese Buddhism is very like the Church of England, both in its weaknesses and virtues.

The thesis of the book requires "Europe" to be a single though growing entity; Christianity and science have always been one, and the only astronomers mentioned are Jesuits. A mention of "Judeo-Christian monotheism" is as much credit as the Semites can expect, especially as the Arabs only copied the Greeks. It all brings comfort because it proves that the whites are genuinely superior. I think that this belief, even if true (it is grotesquely untrue about Chris-tianity), is not likely to do us good, and the mind strays from the doctrine to its preacher. Soon after the war, Koestler felt he hadn't enough petrol, and wrote to the *Partisan Review* "The Labour Party is betraying its trust. I have to bicycle a mile and a half for my groceries. We old-established country squires are being wronged" (or words politically leaving that impression). I had managed to get back to China and had taken on more bicycling than Koestler, so I laughed at this; but no doubt he was reporting a widespread sentiment. Yet again the press shakes with the throbbing bellow of Koestler being wronged: "It's a shame. With all the publicity Zen and Yoga are having, we Christian saints can hardly get on the telly at all." Still, the exposure of Yoga was needed, and there the claim to speak with authority seems justified; and maybe the support for Christianity won't do much harm.

A Happy Few Leap Before Looking

by George Steiner

The problem of artistic and scientific creation, the forward dream of the mind toward insight and invented being, has long fascinated Koestler. The theme crops up in *The Yogi and the Commissar* and in *Insight and Outlook*. It is central to *The Lotus and the Robot* and to the study of Kepler in *The Sleepwalkers*. Now Koestler has made it the subject of a full-scale psychological and historical inquiry, a comparative anatomy of the forward leap.

Whatever its own merits, *The Act of Creation* has a logical place in the career of this fascinating, restless mind. Koestler came of age and stature under the stress of utopian totalitarianism; he experienced personally, and through the witness of his art, complete loss of freedom and the vast sovereignty of death. The core of his work has been a revaluation of the nature of liberty, a hammering out by means of plot and rational argument of the possibilities of free action. It is in the speculative play of the mind, in the power of consciousness to alter the "set" of existence, to surprise itself with revelation, that Koestler now locates the essence of freedom. The underlying design of his work leads from the eclipse of *Darkness at Noon* to the million suns of modern cosmology.

Nearly the whole of this large treatise is an elaboration of Plato's famous proposal that genius (a word in which both creation and growth are etymologically implicit) lies in the ability to juxtapose, to bring into significant relationship areas of experience hitherto disparate. In short, the act of creation is essentially metaphoric. It is the historical circumstance and psychological structure of metaphoric insight which Koestler sets out to analyze.

He starts out with a topic to which increasing attention has been given since Bergson and Freud—the logic and shorthand of wit.

A good joke is like a striking of flints. Springing from the tensed mind, the spark of laughter brings psychological and physiological release. But it does more. The unexpected twist, the verbal association, the reversal of customary values on which a joke is founded, burst open a door of novel understanding. A joke literally has a point. It cuts like an arrow through the cliches and routine of our habitual response. Freud emphasized the ability of humor to act as mask, to bring material otherwise illicit and repressed to the light of awareness in an oblique or disguised way.

Koestler argues that laughter is creative. It results from the collision, deliberate or accidental, of two previously unrelated, apparently contradictory areas of reality, language or attitude. From that collision flashes a brief glimpse of the world newly ordered. Laughter is a "sudden glory" of intelligence; as in a child's game, man regains the faculty of spontaneous action, he says to reality "be otherwise."

In ordinary thought, the mind moves on only one plane. A joke results from the vibrant intersection of habitually incompatible frames of reference. The act of creation occurs when there is *bisociation* (Koestler's key-word), when the mind is in a dual state of imperfect equilibrium. In the process of regaining balance, perception achieves either a *fusion* (the new intellectual syntheses of scientific discovery) or a *confrontation* (the power of art to alter or deepen the focus and values of reality). The scientist formulating a law of motion, the sculptor whose eye reads the form inside the marble, the punster who makes of language a bridge between apparent islands —all are creators. In their act lies the freedom of our condition. And here, by the subtle necessity which governs the lives of those who have broken with communism, Koestler rejoins the metaphysics of Malraux.

The book goes on to explore bisociative patterns in scientific discovery. The *"Eureka"* of Archimedes resulted from a momentary reorientation of focus: "a familiar and unnoticed aspect of a phenomenon—like the rise of the water-level—is suddenly perceived at an unfamiliar and significant angle." Precisely as in a joke, the crust of habit breaks from under our feet, and the mind rights its balance by leaping on to new ground.

But what governs the timing of the intuitive shock? What made

Pythagoras stop in front of a blacksmith's shop and note that metal rods of different lengths gave different sounds under the hammer (the origin of mathematical acoustics, and the study of harmonic series)? There is, says Koestler, a crucial readiness, a gathering of awareness at specific thresholds. Individual minds at various points in a culture become saturated with a problem. The unconscious worries at it like a terrier. Even while attention is relaxed or elsewhere (indeed, particularly then), the current of subterranean thought seeks its goal. Coming into the "field of readiness" a chance incident can act as release. Only if we assume such states of creative latency can we account for the undoubted fact that many scientific discoveries have been made more or less simultaneously by men who had no knowledge of each other's work. The gas was ready for the spark.

After recounting a number of case-histories—Gutenberg, Kepler, Darwin—Koestler seeks to locate the exact role of tangential and subconscious mental activity in the creative leap. He shows that the apparent misdirection, the seeming irrelevance or lapse of consequent argument, can lead to major discovery. He suggests that language, with its built-in routine of order and official logic, can act as a blindfold to the free, creative play of comprehension. Creative thought often uses images or those symbolic patterns and "sensation clusters" which seem to lie deeper than language and move with freer impulse. Even the dim chaos of a dream may reveal creative perspectives closed to the primarily static, commonplace range of waking speech. The inward eye sees more than we can say. As at other points in his writings, Koestler combines a Freudian reading of mental processes with a Jungian topography of the creative unconscious.

"The most important feature of original experimental thinking is the discovery of overlap and agreement where formerly only isolation and difference were recognized." Such discovery depends on a relatively small number of *bisociations,* but also on the presence of a critical mass of accumulated detail and technical potential. A bridge is meaningful if the islands which it links are of some size and strategic location. There has to be a measure of coexistence between individual intuition and available technique.

Even as laughter leads Koestler to a study of the creative collisions of scientific thought, so grief and its mechanism of empathy and release initiate an inquiry into art. He is determined to refute what he takes to be the prevailing dissociation between invention in the arts and in the sciences. In both, the mysterious yet purposeful logic of the unconscious plays a vital part; in both, criteria of elegance, of compactness, of simplicity are highly pertinent to the central truth and validity of the result; both work with intricate, at times semi-automatic, patterns of imagery and chance association.

Above all, there is in both science and art an impulse toward relationship, toward giving to the multiplicity and seeming chaos of experience a living coherence. The scientist has his codes of mathematical and technical inference; the artist expresses his vision of juxtaposed realities through the codes of perspective, rhythm, contrast, key-relations, prosody. Both have to translate vision into an objective medium. The poet and painter, like the great physicist, sees reality in what is, literally, a new light or sequence; he shapes executive form, be it word or pigment, to the new contours of his vision.

Book Two of *The Act of Creation* is primarily technical. It sets out the physiological and psychological foundations of Koestler's theory of the mind. It deals with the growth of the nervous system, with the problem of how attitudes and spontaneities can be transmitted by the genetic code, and with the psycho-social evolution of learning and verbal synthesis. Gathered here are the results of Koestler's life-long interest in neurology and the biological sciences. The work ends with a redefinition of bisociative thought: the creative process has unconscious roots and its logic is oblique and free. But it also has its destructive potential, for it "involves levels of the mind separated by a much wider span than in any other mental activity—except in pathological states." The "strangeness" of the scientist or the frequent infirmity of the artist prepares or reflects the disarray of normal attitudes out of which creation wells. New reality is often built on the ruins of the old. No apple has tasted quite the same since Cezanne: Paul Klee has taught viaducts to walk. But without creation and its risks, man would go chained.

This is as fair a summary as I can give of Koestler's argument. Because of its gray, diffuse style, the book is not easy to read or grasp as a whole. More puzzling is the question—for whom was it written?

Those at all familiar with the field of linguistics, with basic psychology and the history of science will find hardly anything that is new or startling. The notion that creative insight comes of the relocation of reality concepts through collision, reversal or juxtaposition is thoroughly standard. The belief that a new idea is born when (in Lionel Trilling's phrase) two "contradictory emotions are made to confront each other and are required to have a relationship with each other" is commonplace. The examples Koestler gives, the passages he cites from Kohler, Hadamard, Poincare, A. E. Housman, are in numerous anthologies and primers of psychology. The story of Kekule's "dream-discovery" of molecular structure— a text Koestler invokes half a dozen times—is a hoary chestnut and very possibly a literary myth after the fact (the way in which scientists unconsciously shape their autobiographies around certain conventional and literary paradigms is a fascinating subject on which Koestler does not touch).

Indeed, this voluminous treatise shows little interest in what is really new and complex in linguistics, in the analysis of modern logic, and in the more recent work done in the theory of mathematical inference. In his striving for a unified hypothesis, for a psycho-morality of the free intellect, Koestler virtually ignores the differences between relational metaphors in language and in mathematical propositions. Wittgenstein's *Investigations* does not even appear in the bibliography, and hardly anything is said of the crucial problem of the different "responsibilities of metaphor" in ordinary language-statements and in the various grammars of the sciences. Nor does *The Act of Creation* deal with the obscure but vital puzzle of musical invention—an area which may contain decisive clues to the way in which the perception of energy levels and psychic unbalance can be shaped into conscious expression.

Many of the conclusions offered are of disarming banality: "Beauty is a function of truth, truth a function of beauty." This thought, wholly commonplace to anyone who has heard of Poincare, Hardy or Dirac, reflects the fact that in even the most abstruse scientific formulation, elegance and comeliness of solution are likely symptoms of validity (but not always, and it is the exceptions that challenge inquiry). Where Koestler becomes "technical," in the use of special vocabulary and graphs, the effect is often unsophisticated. What evidence is there that biochemistry comes higher than chemistry on a curve of "verifiable objectivity" (in fact, is this a meaningful statement at all)?

Perhaps the best way to judge this book is to regard it as *haute vulgarisation,* a popularization and summation of certain aspects of aesthetics, psychology and the history of science. Those who have not read such works as Newman's *World of Mathematics,* Gombrich's *Art and Illusion* or Koestler's own previous accounts of cosmological discovery, will find classic material set out with authority. The latter sections of the argument give a valuable exposition of recent advances in genetics and neuro-physiology.

The Act of Creation, in short, represents Koestler as a middle-man between science and the general public. It is an important function and he has exercised it brilliantly throughout his career as a writer. Whether many general readers will, in fact, labor through this work or whether it will invite rereading, is more doubtful. But whatever the success of the present instance, the author of *Darkness at Noon* has often put each of us in his debt.

The Metaphysics of Arthur Koestler

by Henry David Aiken

When this extraordinary book—part treatise and part biology and psychology copy book, part independent scientific speculation and part romantic *Naturphilosophie*—was published in England earlier this year, it caused something of a sensation. No one quite knew how to take it. Some reviewers (and it was reviewed profusely and often at great length) professed to think that, however improbably, *The Act of Creation* is itself a true act of scientific creation, conceivably the greatest and certainly the most ambitious work in the life sciences since Darwin's epochal *Origin of Species*. On the other side, perhaps misled by Koestler's reputation as a novelist (it is not without significance that Koestler has been mainly a political novelist for whom the work of imaginative literature may be at the same time a moral and political act), by his inappropriately lively and witty style, by displays of subjective reactions presumably irrelevant to questions of objective scientific understanding and truth, and by his bland refusal to be daunted by any intellectual problem, no matter how technical or complex, many were unable to take him seriously in the role of scientist. In their view, Koestler does not fully realize what is involved in scientific inquiry, and his book, for all its learning, must be judged as the misplaced product of an incurably poetic imagination. Yet on both sides of the controversy, the critics seemed uncertain of their own reactions, and before they were through they had usually managed to hedge their bets by radical, if piecemeal, concessions to the opposing point of view.

I scarcely blame them. For one thing, *The Act of Creation* contains not one but two (no doubt related) books of very different ranges, perspectives, and styles. The first is beautifully readable and, for

"The Metaphysics of Arthur Koestler," by Henry David Aiken. From *The New York Review of Books*, III (December 17, 1964), 22-25. Copyright © 1964 by Henry David Aiken. Reprinted by permission of Henry David Aiken.

the most part, intelligible to any informed twentieth-century reader; the other is highly technical, occasionally unintelligible except to specialists and sometimes (I suspect) not even to them, but at the same time immensely ranging, not to say visionary, in its purview. For another thing, both books, for all their differences, have similar defects. Here I am not speaking of factual errors, most of which could no doubt be removed without affecting the main drift of Koestler's arguments. The underlying difficulty concerns the intention of the book as a whole. What is Koestler really up to? Would it be an egregious mistake to take the book at its face value? But, then, what precisely is its face value? Practicing scientists will be, have been, disposed to dismiss Koestler as a possibly gifted but presumptuous and uncritical "writer" who has wandered unaccountably into a field for which, by training and aptitude, he is intrinsically unfitted. Literary men, especially those who have erected a wall between "imaginative literature" and other forms of writing, whether scientific, historical, criticial, or philosophical will "submit" that Koestler is at once making clear at the theoretical level what was always apparent from his practice, namely, that he is not an artist but an artificer, a maker and joiner who has been filling in time while his story-teller's imagination has lain fallow. Either way, it seems impossible to accept his book as a "normal" contribution to biological and psychological science. And the point is merely sharpened by Professor Sir Cyril Burt's statement, in an admiring if cautious Foreword, that Koestler had a scientific education, has "visited" in many places of learning where serious psychological research is conducted, has a formidable knowledge of the "literature" of the subject, and enjoys the intimate friendship of some of the most original investigators in contemporary science, "from nuclear physics to experimental neurology."

To complete the picture, Koestler himself has created further uncertainty by a rather testy and cryptic reply to one reviewer who had made the important point, which others have also noted, that Koestler not only does not adequately distinguish, but apparently fails to appreciate, the salient difference between the scientist's original moment of insight or discovery and the objective validation of his hypothesis, and between his (the scientist's) "moment of truth" and the achievement of public scientific knowledge. Even if, as

Koestler contends, there is in all human thought a continuous gradient from "objective" to "subjective" reactions, this does not prove what Koestler evidently thinks it proves. For scientific objectivity concerns, not a characteristic response on the part of scientific discoverers, whether "subjective" or "objective," but conformity to a system of impersonal practices for testing hypotheses. If Koestler were willing to concede this, his two main arguments could still be true: that the scientist's original insight bears a close analogy to the artist's creative act; and that certain psychological (and ultimately physiological) conditions are common to them both. Why is he unwilling to make this saving concession which would seem to leave his theory of creation virtually intact? This question, I believe, is but one side of a more general question about the nature of his achievement. What no one seems to have asked is this: why does Koestler always stretch the range of his ideas to, and beyond, the breaking point? And what is the source of his passion for melding attitudes or temperaments? These questions are not answered by the charge that he lacks scientific discipline or that he suffers from the artist's supposed incapacity for handling general ideas. When he chooses, Koestler can be as restrained and as analytical as the most proper academic scientists. Nor is he lacking in self-criticism. He makes clear at the outset that he has "no illusions about the prospects of the theory....it will suffer the inevitable fate of being proven wrong in many, or most, details....What I am hoping for is that it will be found to contain a shadowy pattern of truth, and that it may stimulate those who search for unity in the diverse manifestations of human thought and emotion." Moreover, as it seems to me, Koestler is quite right in contending that there is no such thing as *the* artistic or *the* scientific temperament. The ideas both of art and of science concern forms, not of temperament, but of achievement. And to either form of achievement there is no one temperamental throughway. In my judgment, the real source of Koestler's "defects" as a scientist is, rather, an overriding concern, not fully appreciated either by himself or by his critics, which can only be called metaphysical. And it is as metaphysics that *The Act of Creation* as a whole must be judged. However, before I can even begin to suggest why, and how, this is so, we must first take a closer look at his theory itself.

The Act of Creation is, I believe, a more truly creative work than any of Koestler's novels and a more adequate revelation both of his powers as a writer and of his enduring interests as a man. In his own view, however, Koestler the quondam novelist and Koestler the scientific psychologist are merely chips off the same block. According to him, the creative faculty in whatever form is owing to a circumstance which he calls "bisociation." And we recognize this intuitively whenever we laugh at a joke, are dazzled by a fine metaphor, are astonished and excited by a unification of styles, or "see," for the first time, the possibility of a significant theoretical breakthrough in a scientific inquiry. In short, one touch of genius — or bisociation — makes the whole world kin. Or so Koestler believes. And why should this not be so? That one man is tone deaf and another good at numbers, or that one has an eye for facts and another is impervious to them proves nothing to the contrary. Koestler is talking about — if he will forgive the word — the fundamental mechanism of genius, not the specific "skills," native or acquired, that may be necessary to particular acts of creation. On this score, he merely underlines a point we all must have known before, namely, that it is not the skill or facility that makes the creative artist or scientist, but what he does with it. In short, Koestler is interested in that transfiguring movement of the mind which turns cleverness into the creative act and talent into the stroke of genius. He believes that he can define the essential conditions of that movement. He also thinks, perhaps incontinently, that its more primitive analogues are in evidence everywhere in the organic world.

The theory of bisociation is explained and profusely illustrated at the human level in the lengthy but continuously fascinating first book of *The Act of Creation*. Here Koestler is at his ease. He entertains while he enlightens and persuades, and even though one may not really be shown in the end just why a bisociative act occurs in one situation but not in another, one is nonetheless enabled virtually to "see" Gutenberg in the act of inventing the printing press, Kepler (always a special hero of Koestler's) in the process of discovering his three great laws of planetary motion, and Darwin moving up to and then lighting upon, as Darwin himself put it, "the long-sought-for law of nature that solved the problem of the origin of the species." Technically, "bisociation" may best be understood by distinguishing it from unitary, habitual associations on a single "plane" of experience. Connections of the latter sort, involving merely the articulation of an established routine, are manifest in such standard examples as, say, the association of clouds with rain, of lox with bagels, of the word "Fido" with Fido. Bisociation, on the contrary, occurs only when a *new* connection is made between two (or more) independent contexts of association which Koestler variously calls "frames of reference," "universes of discourse," or "types of logic."[1]

Koestler shrewdly introduces his study of bisociation through an account of humor which, although (in my judgment) too intellectualistic, is one of the most convincing parts of his book. Humorous bisociation involves the perception of a situation in two habitually incompatible associative contexts. This "causes" an abrupt transfer of the train of thought from one "frame of reference" to another governed, as he puts it, by "a different logic or 'rule of the game.' " In humor, however, certain emotions, "owing to their greater inertia," cannot follow such rapid intellectual moves and so, "discarded by reason, they are worked off along channels of least resistance in laughter." The emotions involved are, in particular, those of the self-assertive, aggressive-defensive type, which are based on the sympathetic-adrenal system and tend to beget bodily activity. "Laughter is a luxury reflect which could arise only in a creature whose reason has gained a degree of autonomy from the urges of emotion, and enables him to perceive his own emotions as

[1] Here, I may add, Koestler seems to remind us of the post-Wittgensteinian linguistic philosophers who treat each distinct "form of words" as having a characteristic "logic" of its own; the crucial difference here is that Koestler, in limiting himself to bisociations of frames of *reference,* fails to perceive possibilities of verbal bisociation that may arise from the collision or fusion of whole frames of reference with, say, "frames" of expressive or emotive meaning. In fact, my guess is that an adequate account of humor and of artistic creation, as distinct from the account of scientific discovery, would require just such cross-frame bisociations. Curiously, the "romantic" Koestler is often too narrowly intellectualistic in his approach to modes of bisociation. And one reason for this may well be, ironically, that his own training was scientific rather than humanistic and literary. I suggest, however, that an adequate analysis of metaphor and of rhetoric would require a more systemic study than Koestler gives of non-referential and non-descriptive forms of expression. Perhaps this may also help to explain why Koestler limits his morphology of human-creativity to the jester, the scientist, and the artist, leaving out of account the religious genius, the prophet, the moralist, and the charismatic leader.

redundant—to realize that he has been fooled." There is no space
to cite a fair sample of the many jokes and witicisms (both good
and bad) which Koestler so perceptively and convincingly analyzes.
Consider the following "memorable statement" which appeared
(ye gods!) in *Vogue:*

> Belsen and Buchenwald have put a stop to the too-thin woman age,
> to the cult of undernourishment.

This horror, as Koestler says, "makes one shudder, yet it is funny
in a ghastly way, foreshadowing the 'sick jokes' of a later decade.
The idea of starvation is bisociated with one tragic, and another,
utterly trivial, context." The result, in spite of ourselves, is an un-
controllable titter. Let me add only that here, above all, it is not
just *ideas* that are bisociated, but whole ideo-motor-affective *Ges-
talten* of which the "idea" provides merely the nucleus.

Scientific discovery also involves the same bisociation of "matrices."
(This is the technical term that Koestler uses in referring more
generally to the standardized routines, frames, abilities, skills,
etc. that are governed by sets of rules or, as he calls them, "codes.")
The difference lies in the fact that in science we find "a blend of
passions in which both the self-asserting and self-transcending tendencies participate—symbolized by the Mad Professor and the
Benevolent Magician of folk lore." Here, however, both tendencies
are sublimated and each is offset by the other. This development,
Koestler argues, is foreshadowed in the exploratory behavior of
"clever animals" like the chimpanzee which, in Köhler's classic
experiment, discovered, after many unsuccessful efforts, that he
could rake a banana into his cage by fitting two short hollow sticks
together. The chimp's original motivation was to get the banana,
but his new discovery "pleased him so immensely" that he kept
repeating the trick and forgot to eat it. "Eureka!" he would no doubt
have said had he possessed that verbal skill, "I have it!" For Koestler in fact Archimedes' transfixed cry expresses the archetypal
jubilation of all intellectual discoverers.

Koestler's account of artistic creativity is no less intriguing than
his discussions of creativity in humor and in science. He begins with
an explanation of what he calls "the logic of the moist eye" in which
he contrasts with great skill the underlying responses involved in
comedy and tragedy. But this is merely preliminary to a complex

and subtle treatment of forms of verbal and visual creation (here one wonders whether it was merely the pressure of time that is responsible for the salient omission of an extended discussion of music, which is at once the formal and the expressive art, *par excellence*). It must suffice to say that, in Koestler's view, whereas laughter is sparked by the collision of matrices, and scientific discovery by their integration, aesthetic activity arises from a "juxtaposition" of matrices in which there occurs an emotional catharsis, that is, "the rise, expansion, and ebbing away of the self-transcending emotions." Here, also, however, there is a characteristic insistence upon *"intellectual illumination*—seeing something familiar in a new light...." The emotional catharsis simply *follows* the bisociative intellectual illumination. To my mind, the arch-foe of mechanistic theories in psychology and biology has himself fallen into a rather mechanistic view of the role of emotion in art. I would suggest both that emotion is present *in* the bisociative confrontation and that pre-established forms of emotional reactions by themselves be at least central aspects of the artist's creative act.

There is no space for adequate resumé of *Book Two* (entitled *Habit and Originality*) which sets out the general bio-psychological theory of which the theory of human creativity developed in *Book One* is, in principle, merely a special, if also to most of us the most interesting and important case. As Koestler puts it, whereas *Book One* represents an "upward approach" that moves from part to whole and examines the creative act in its most complex human forms, *Book Two* represents a "downward approach" that moves from the complex to the elementary and from the whole to its parts. Thus, if Koestler is right, *The Act of Creation* represents the meshing of a novel theory of man's highest mental processes into a universal thesis which applies to, and in principle helps to "explain," certain patterns of change to be found in *all* forms of life "from embryonic development to symbolic thinking." All such processes of development are "governed" by certain "rules of the game" which give them appearance of purpose. Whether phylogenetically or ontogenetically acquired, these rules, or "codes" as Koestler calls them, operate on all levels of life. And on all levels, there occur creative "fusions" or "marriages" (bisociations) of such coded routines, skills, or matrices.

As one perhaps might have anticipated, the basic model of the creative act is sexual reproduction. Here, I am bound to say, it is not easy to know how far fact leads figure, or figure fact. Koestler not only uses his models; he so pulls and hauls them, partly by metaphorical and analogical extension, partly by contextual re-definition, that one does not always know in the end what illuminates and what is being illuminated. In any case, Koestler is *not* suggesting, I take it, that sex is actually the source of all creative advances in the organic world. And while there are echoes of, as well as many references to, Freud (and to a lesser extent Jung) in the book, it would be a radical mistake to suppose either that Koestler is a Freud gone mad or that he is offering a kind of quasi- or pseudo-analytic account of creation of the sort one might expect from a freely bisociating psychological novelist. On the contrary, the whole bent of Koestler's approach is in direct conflict with the mechanistic side of a theory of development which would explain all mature forms of human behavior in terms of certain infantile or pre-natal fixations.

The old fashioned notion of organic hierarchies is fundamental to Koestler's "general theory." Roughly, his contention is that any complex organism is an hierarchial system of units, subunits, sub-sub-units, and so on. However, an organic hierarchy is not simply an "order of rank" of the sort exhibited in the "pecking hierarchy" of the farm yard. As in the case of a military organization with its squads, platoons, companies, etc., each unit in an organic hierarchy possesses a certain wholeness and autonomy, although each lower order unit is also subordinate to that just above it in the hierarchy to which it belongs. In individual organisms, Koestler believes, such hierarchical organization is exhibited not only in their main organs, but also in their cells and cell parts. Moreover, on every level, there are at work, according to him, "homologous" principles, so that any activity or process at one level has its homologue at every other level. In fact, all higher-order mental processes have their lower-order bodily equivalents and vice versa. Koestler thus claims that the "dichotomy" of "self-assertion and participation" holds on all levels of bodily action and reaction, and, conversely, that to every form of "bodily" self-maintenance and self-repair there is a corresponding higher "mental" homologue. Somewhat perplexingly, however, homologous principles are evidently thought to apply not only within hierarchies internal to individual organisms but also across species to the great hierarchy of natural organic kinds. Thus, for example, in the "general alarm reactions" of injured animals there occurs something very like the "stress" undergone by artists and scientists in the act of creation.

Koestler goes very far with such comparisons. Indeed, such verbal phenomena as rhythm and rhyme, assonance and pun are even said to be "vestigial echoes" of the "primitive pulsations of living matter." These remarks, apart from any question about their *sense,* plainly show Koestler's inability to limit the application of his notion of organic hierarchies. The result is that we find ourselves in increasing doubt as to what a genuine hierarchical organization or connection really is. I can understand, for instance, how in principle a cell-part can be viewed as standing in a homologous hierarchical relation to the cell to which it belongs, but not, so help me, if I am asked to think of such a relation as holding between verbal rhythms and "primitive pulsations of living matter"—whatever they are.

Here, I believe, is a type of difficulty that is both recurrent in and symptomatic of Koestler's thought: Having formulated what looks to be a significant concept or thesis he then stretches it so far and applies it so loosely that a question is eventually raised both about its own rules of meaning and about the sort of game Koestler is playing with it. And, in a word, he has a way of driving an idea so far into the ground that it seems to lose its point; or else, to follow his own analogy, he shoots it so far into the air that it simply passes beyond the range of our intellectual vision. This is a great pity, not so much because it raises doubts about Koestler's discipline as a scientific thinker (similar doubts can be raised about many if not most seminal minds in science), but also, and more importantly, it makes it much harder than necessary to do justice to the main drift of his thinking. One has constantly to remind oneself that the unfruitfulness of a particular analogy does not entail the failure of analogical thinking as such, and that the misapplication of a theory is indeed a misapplication only, and not necessarily an evidence against the theory. On the other side, it is essential to realize that questions of success and failure in such matters are entirely relative to the degree of precision with which concepts are defined and theories formulated. What would be an absurd misapplication of a theory in mathematical physics may be merely suggestive in biology; what seems anomolous in biochemistry may be splendidly analogical in political "science" or theology. Concepts applied with a certain precision to the sphere of human action may have no meaning or else have to be radically redefined, when applied for scientific purposes within the domains of physics and chemistry.

The key phrase in the preceding sentence is of course "for scientific purposes." Where our task is not, as in physical science, to describe and to predict phenomena, but, as in metaphysics, to give a unifying sense of the lay of the land, or, as in theology, to prepare a unifying basis for worship or a direction for the devotional intent, such lack of precision, or such misapplication, may be harmless or even exciting. Why *not* say that one touch of nature makes the whole world kin if the point in saying it is to bring Achilles out of his tent? Why not call the principle of creation a Father, a bisociative secretion, or a swerve in the matrix of life, if *that* moves, or comforts, or helps the human spirit itself to "bisociate," to analogize, to think and feel in ways that are truly life-enhancing.

As William James would say, I am in some sense on Koestler's side against those who suppose that the concepts of the reflex, the routine, the skill, the method, and the institution provide adequate bases, or models, for the understanding of human life or of nature. Man betrays himself when he "reduces" himself to a system of routines, to a creature who simply "adapts" himself to "situations" by skills already available to him. Koestler is on the side of freedom and life, or at any rate the good life, and freedom are deeply intertwined. Still, I am not sure that Koestler will be pleased by my favor. For even if his theories on certain reaches turn out to have explanatory value, they are not, as they stand, scientific theories. Or so it seems to me. What, then, are they? Fundamentally, the role of the theories of bisociation and of organic heirarchies, not to say, of their union, is metaphysical. Now of course old-line positivists will regard this as equivalent to a charge that Koestler's theories are essentially meaningless. But this charge holds only for scientific reference and verification. I have said, partly in criticism of Koestler himself, that he is too much beholden to the model of the frame of *reference*. He really does seem to think that the jester is simply one who laughs off his bisociative "discovery" and that the artist is one who drains his "discovery" (shades of Aristotle, whom Koestler abominates) into an emotional catharsis. This is a mistake. The point, however, is that there are forms of thought-feeling-action, and forms of expression that subtend them, which do not have a "discovery," at least in the scientific sense, as the consummation to be wished. Koestler's theses are truly creative, but they are creative in the metaphysical rather than in the scientific dimension: that is to say, they are fresh, exciting principles of orientation that suggest approaches to a *Weltanschauung* which I find exhilarating to contemplate. Their "verification" is not so much perceptual as emotional-volitional. Here, so to say, is not a thesis, but a vision, not a theory, but a unifying picture which, in an age of specialization, of bifucations — and walls — is a refreshment of the soul. One touch of genius may indeed make the whole world kin. Let us see.

Toward the Freudian Pill

by Leslie Fiedler

The title of Arthur Koestler's most recent book[1] seems to me
terrifyingly apt in a way he did not intend; for he himself is, and
has long been, a ghost: the ghost of a man who died when his God
failed. But I continue to read him—strain to hear the words he
brings back from the Other Side and speaks from the shadowy
periphery of the world at whose centre I am still condemned to
live. It is because, I suppose, I believe in ghosts, even the ghosts of
departed journalists; and piety constrains me to attend especially
to one who was my teacher before he died. That I learned much
from *Darkness at Noon* and *Scum of the Earth* and Koestler's contribution to *The God that Failed,* I have no wish to deny, indeed,
find special pleasure in acknowledging. Koestler helped to deliver
me from the platitudes of the Thirties, from those organised self-
deceptions which, being my first, were especially dear and difficult
to escape.

Nonetheless, I am—perhaps for that very reason—all the more
dismayed to find the wisdom of those early works, once central to
the experience of the young, re-echoed with a dying fall at a moment when it has come to seem offensively irrelevant. Bound to
recapitulate the moment of terror attendant on their taking off,
ghosts are inevitably bores. And such a bore Koestler proves himself, when, approaching the climax of his book, he cannot resist
quoting (for publication in 1967) his own words written in 1954
about his encounter with Stalinism in the Thirties:

> By setting up this automatic sorting machine in his mind, it was still
> possible in 1933 for a European to live in Russia and yet remain a

"Toward the Freudian Pill," by Leslie Fiedler. From *The New Statesman and
Nation,* LXXIV (October 27, 1967), 548-549. Reprinted by permission of The New
Statesman and Nation Publishing Company Ltd.

[1][*The Ghost in the Machine* (London: Hutchinson & Co., 1967).—Ed.].

> Communist.... The Communist mind has perfected the techniques of self-deception in the same manner as its techniques of mass propaganda.

Etc. Etc. But we need no ghost come back from the dead to tell us this.

Nor do we need to be informed once more about the limitations of orthodox Freudianism, nor those of Behavioural Psychology as defined between 1913 and 1928 by J. B. Watson. Yet Koestler cannot stay away from these subjects—his essential quarrel being with the end of the 19th century and the first decades of ours. To be sure, he manages to talk about B. F. Skinner and the more contemporary developments of behaviorism; but this is largely, one feels, out of a desire to prove (especially to himself) that he is not merely a beater of dead horses. Indeed, there is a special index to his book called "On Not Flogging Dead Horses," in which Koestler (nettled by such charges against *The Act of Creation,* which along with the present volume and *The Sleepwalkers* constitutes a trilogy) argues that the horses he flogs cannot really be dead, since some men still ride them. And once more there is the compulsive allusion to Stalinism ("The Soviet Government, during the years of Stalin's rule, committed barbarities on an equal scale..."). But in the land of the dead, quite obviously there are dead riders as well as dead floggers of dead beasts; and though in a pinch one would choose the floggers over the riders, best of all would be to be spared both.

To be sure, Koestler does refer occasionally to the world of the living, which is to say, the world of the young, to whom Stalin and J. B. Watson, along with Hitler and Freud, are figures quite as historically remote as Akhnaton or Napoleon; and he even cites a couple of sentences from J. B. S. Haldane in a chapter called "Evolution CTD: Undoing and Redoing" which might well have led him to the realisation that more and more the world which all of us, young or old, inhabit is precisely the world of the young. Haldane's insight is worth lingering over:

> If human evolution is to continue along the same lines as in the past, it will probably involve still greater prolongation of childhood and retardation of maturity. Some of the characters distinguishing adult man will be lost.

But Koestler does not pause to reflect on the implication of an observation that, physiologically as well as psychologically, sociologically, mythically, youth rather than maturity is destined to become man's fate — and that this change may well represent the essential human transcendance of our animal beginnings.

The problem seems to be that Koestler is moved by a scarcely concealed hatred and resentment of the young, the envy — one is tempted to say — of the dead for the living. What else can explain the sheer nastiness, compounded by arrogant superficiality, of his offhand remark about "the hordes of screaming teenage Bacchantae mobbing Popstars, and the leering teen-age Narcissi coiffured like cockroaches." Popular Culture is for Koestler as utterly contempible as the young who produce and consume it; though in fact it can be argued that his own book represents precisely the assimilation of science to that Popular Culture. Searching for the ultimately pejorative epithet he is as likely as not to find it in the word "Pop." In one place, at any rate, he speaks of the "Pop-Nirvana" imagined by Aldous Huxley, and in another, of the "perversions of Pop-Zen" in the works of Suzuki. Huxley and Suzuki, however, are among the very few thinkers alluded to by Koestler who appeal at all to the sort of young men and women for whom the writers he admires or on whom he vents his spite scarcely exist at all.

If he has read any of the more recent sages and gurus who speak to them as Marx and Freud spoke to the young of his generation — Marshall McLuhan, Buckminster Fuller, Ronald Laing, Norman O. Brown, Timothy Leary, for instance — he certainly does not mention them; yet the last three at least, deal centrally with an essential problem of our times which Koestler himself unexpectedly confronts. For there is, finally, in his book something living and new: not the Pop Science, to be sure, with its solemn mystifications and magic formulae disguised as definitions —

> …multi-levelled hierarchies of semi-autonomous sub-wholes branching into sub-wholes of a lower order…intermediate entities which, relative to their subordinates in the hierarchy, function as self-contained wholes: relative to their superordinates as dependent parts…

Recited under the proper conditions, this might serve to evoke a minor demon or two, quite like the similar jargon intoned in the rat-running laboratories whose presiding witchdoctors Koestler affects to dispise. But even backed up with bell, book and candle, it cannot exorcise that great devil of irrationality whom Koestler believes is haunting our world. Yet an act of exorcism rather than one of evocation is what Koestler clearly intends—convinced, like many another guilt-ridden deicide, that it is his duty to destroy those demons who have, disconcertingly, survived his gods.

As a matter of fact, Koestler himself knows quite well that words, though they may kill gods, cannot annihilate devils. "Like the reader," he confesses as he prepares to conclude, "I would prefer to set my hopes on moral persuasion by word and example. But we are a mentally sick race, and as such deaf...." And so he turns to pharmacology, the use of mind-altering drugs, as a last desperate hope. And here, at last, he has entered the living world, *materialised*, as the spiritualists say of their apparitions. How familiar, even fashionable, are the very terms he employs: we must turn to "the Pill" to achieve a "Final Revolution"; we must strive for the "beneficial mutation" of our species, otherwise doomed because of an imbalance between the archaic, instinctive part of the brain and the newer, more rational part. It might well be Leary himself speaking, or—to turn to the despised world of Pop-music, the Mothers of Invention, who inscribed on the jacket of their album, "Freak Out," the slogan: JOIN THE UNITED MUTATIONS.

At the very least, he seems to be seconding his own contemporary, Aldous Huxley, who, in *The Gates of Perception* and *Heaven and Hell,* foresaw a situation, a dilemma, of whose meanings some of us even now are less aware than he was then. But Koestler hastens to assure us that he profoundly disagrees with Huxley's advocacy of "mescalin and other psychodelic drugs"—and his misspelling of the word "psychedelic," so recently invented but already so familiar, tells us even more than his statement itself about where, in the peripheral shadows, he continues to stand. Or perhaps Koestler has mis-written it deliberately as one mis-speaks the name of an antagonist one pretends to despise. But to write "psychodelic" with conscious intent as a snide reference perhaps to the mad protagonist of Alfred Hitchcock's thriller is to compound the offence. That the New Revolution, the latest Final Combat has moved from the larger world to the smaller and will be settled, with the aid of psycho-

chemistry, inside our skulls he knows very well. But he has de
clared his allegiance to the Other Side from that on which such
new prophets as Norman O. Brown and R. D. Laing have taken a
stand—favouring not the release of the repressed archaic in us,
but the restoration of a "hierarchic order," in which thought and
emotion are to be united under the hegemony of thought. It is the
old Freudian song set to a new tune: the hope that where *id* was
ego will be—with the help of a Pill this time around, since the
Couch has failed. But, alas, all the Pills invented or rediscovered
so far are on the side of the *id*; the Freudian Pill remains still a
dream.

The Book of Arthur

by Stephen Toulmin

What do we demand of Science? Vitamin-reinforced bread and astronautical circuses; *Genesis* according to Hoyle and the *Revelations* of Teilhard the Divine; piecemeal, tentative theories about those aspects of nature that we can now bring into focus; or a bit of all three? That question must not be answered in a hurry. For all three ambitions—technological, theological, and philosophical—have been operative throughout the development of scientific thought, and its history could be written with an eye to the changing balance between them.

Certainly, technology has been the junior partner in the alliance. The mask of Francis Bacon has always concealed the face of Isaac Newton, and has been used by scientists to catch patrons for their excursions into philosophy and theology. (Recall how the newly hatched Royal Society elected as its Secretary Samuel Pepys of Charles II's Admiralty, and how today's National Science Foundation was incubated beforehand within the Office of Naval Research.) Though always a selling point, technology has, intellectually speaking, never come near to the heart of science. For that one must look rather at the other two strands: the piecemeal, tentative aim well captured in Karl Popper's formula, *Conjectures and Refutations,* of conceiving and criticizing hypothetical solutions to specific theoretical problems; and the more comprehensive, speculative aim, of fitting these theoretical concepts together into an all-embracing—and, if possible, a humanly significant—view of the world.

Many tough-minded scientists (it is true) dislike having science linked with theology even more than with technology, regarding their tender-minded colleagues' effusions about Creation, or design, or freewill, as a mark of soft-centeredness for which Science her-

"The Book of Arthur," by Stephen Toulmin. From *The New York Review of Books,* X (April 11, 1968), 16-21. Copyright © Nyrev, Inc. Reprinted by permission of *The New York Review of Books.*

self (Hagia Sophia) is in no way responsible. Still: from the time of
Newton until barely a century ago, the theological aims of science
were accepted as co-equal with its theoretical aims, so that "natural
theology" was an institutionalized element in the scientific enterprise itself. When, for instance, the Royal Society sponsored publication of the *Bridgewater Treatises* (on "the Power, Wonder, and
Goodness of God, as manifested in the Creation") nobody questioned
that this was a proper function for a scientific academy. Natural
theology has become wholly "disestablished" from the kingdom of
·science only in the twentieth century.

Even now, there are those who deplore the new order of things.
In different ways, such men as Michael Polanyi and Julian Huxley,
Arthur Koestler and Teilhard de Chardin all express regret at the
severance of "natural philosophy" from the discussion of *Weltanschauungen*. All of them let their intellectual imaginations roam
beyond the established results of disciplined scientific research,
into cloudier regions of speculation—about *Personal Knowledge* as
a clue to the Divine, about a religion based on Science rather than
Revelation, or about a "Christogenesis" which shall be the apotheosis
of both biological and human history. The appearance of the final
installment of the vast trilogy that has occupied Arthur Koestler for
the last ten years, or more, is an occasion for reassessing the new
situation.

Intellectual courage and imagination on this scale are, in themselves, rare and admirable; but has there not been something mis-
guided about the whole thing? Faced with Koestler's attempt to
bring the concepts of the different sciences into a synthetic unity,
for the sake of a general Vision of Nature that will illuminate the
Glory and Predicament of Man, we must ask: "Were there not in
fact strong reasons, both sociological and intellectual, why scientific
theory was divorced from natural theology in the first place—
reasons that still hold?"

Before turning to the actual substance of Koestler's completed
trilogy, we must recall the hurdles he has set himself to clear. First,
the institutional hurdle: the chief sociological mark of twentieth-
century Science is the fact that it has become a profession, and the
structure of scientific institutions today simply reflects this. For they
are required, as never before, to be the instruments of coherent

professional disciplines. That demand, by itself, has imposed on Science a new and sharper boundary, dividing a central class of problems and hypotheses, observations and experiments—whose very specificity and close relation to experience makes them the collective concern of all the scientists involved—from a peripheral class of speculative theses about the "broader implications and tendencies" of the sciences—over which there is no hope of exercising the strict rational control expected within a scientific discipline.

Thus, working as a biologist, Julian Huxley has contributed to our understanding of evolution (small "e"), in ways his professional colleagues have been able to check for themselves, by seeing how his hypotheses fare in competition with their rivals, when compared with the records of our experience. Yet Huxley has been anxious to develop also a world-view embracing all cosmic history: an optimistic cosmogony in which Evolution (capital "E") becomes the central theme of History—linking primeval "pre-biotic" slime to modern democratic society, by way of all the intervening "emergent" phrases of organic descent—and which at the same time will provide the ultimate justification for our moral codes, in the form of an *Evolutionary Ethics*. At this point, the problem of rational control becomes acute. To Thomas Henry Huxley, Julian's grandfather, it was equally clear that Ethics and Evolution headed not in the same direction, but in directly opposite directions: moral action should not promote organic evolution, but should suspend and counteract its brutalities. How was one to choose between T. H.'s views and Julian's? Scientifically speaking, one couldn't; for, scientifically, there was no basis for a choice between them. In moving from questions about the specific operations of organic evolution to questions about the relevance of Evolution to Ethics, they had crossed the boundary separating the hypotheses of science itself from its speculative "implications"; and in the process the whole character of the questions at issue had changed.

The establishment of this sharper boundary has had one healthy effect: it has made scientists intellectually responsive to one another's judgments, not only about the doctrines they are ready to assert, but—more important—also over the questions about which rational judgment must be for the moment suspended, in this respect they have gone beyond Socrates, for whom maturity lay in the personal acknowledgment of all that he did not know, to the position of Cusanus. Wisdom lies, for them, in the institutionalization of ignorance.

This first hurdle by itself need not be entirely daunting. The fact that the institutionalized disciplines of Science no longer find room for natural theology leaves us free to consider the broader significance of scientific ideas and insights as individuals—though it demands that we do so with proper cautions and qualifications. We are not compelled, as individuals, to act like those intellectual ascetics (and they include many working scientists) for whom the prattle of implication-hunters is as the crackling of thorns under a pot. But there is a further, intellectual hurdle, whose consequences can be more serious. Unless we are absolutely scrupulous in our handling of the ideas we pick up, our discussions of the "implications" of Science can be seriously misleading, and run into cross-purposes with the scientific debate itself. There is a standard historical illustration of this point that is directly relevant to Koestler's new book.

Our contemporary physics and physiology have developed from the New Mechanical Philosophy of Descartes and Newton; their systems were attacked during the eithteenth century both by Leibniz and by Goethe. The two attacks were quite different in character. Leibniz argued—as a matter of systematic theory—against the Cartesians' determination to explain the operation of "ordered systems" by their structure, material composition, and mechanisms alone. This attempt, he declared, inevitably distracts us from the "ordering principles" according to which the continuity and patterns of action of such systems need to be understood. Cartesian physiologists, for instance, tried to explain the passions and emotions shared by men and the lower animals as a mechanical effect of the "agitated motions" of the separate "material particles" making up our bodies and brains; and similarly for all other physiological operations of animal organs and organisms. In Leibniz's view, such a theoretical program is radically defective since, in concentrating on the component "particles," it fails entirely to explain the unity and individuality of the systems—their character as "monads." (In twentieth-century jargon: Leibniz argued that the "integrative" action of ordered systems must be understood, not by considering them as material structures alone, but in terms of the functions and activities that are characteristic of the entire "monadic" systems.)

If we now look for labels to contrast Descartes' and Leibniz's methodologies, we may (if we please) call them "mechanicist" and "organicist" respectively; but, since this was a critical debate *within* natural philosophy, the labels must—emphatically—have a small "m" and "o." Leibniz was no more inclined than Descartes to place limits on the scope of mechanistic analysis. Clearly (he said) there must be brain-processes paralleling our mental experiences and activities, to whatever degree of detail we care to probe; it is just that taking all these processes individually, and explaining their mechanical operations, leave the intrinsic character of perception and thought, as activities of the entire man, unaffected and unexplained.

Goethe and Schiller attacked from a very different angle. In their eyes, Newtonian Science was not just intellectually deficient but anathema. As they saw it, Newton had represented all material things as "blind impoverished mechanisms," and had denied the "rich purposive creativity" of living, thinking, feeling, beings:

> Like the dead strokes of a pendulum-clock
> Nature, bereft of all her Divinities,
> Slavishly serves the Law of Gravitation.

Any natural science worked out on the mechanical principles followed by Descartes and Newton—even, to be truthful, by Leibniz— must be subordinated to a broader organic vision of Nature; and the scope of mechanistic analysis must be explicitly curtailed. So Goethe the Romantic Prophet preached Organicism, in direct opposition to *all* the mathematically based programs of the New Philosophers, whom he denounced as collectively committed to a Mechanicist world-view.

Evidently, there was room here for a plain misunderstanding, just so long as the philosophical and theological strands in Science were not handled separately. Merely because natural philosophers from Descartes on had concentrated on developing and testing mechanical hypotheses about the workings of nature, they were not necessarily committed—either collectively or individually—to a

Mechanicist view. Nor has there been any very consistent correlation between a man's intellectual methods within Science and the theological framework in which he has, personally, interpreted the broader significance of his own ideas. (Notoriously, Faraday was a Sandemanian.) With all affection and respect, one must insist that — over this point — Goethe was sadly confused.

All this has to be said in preface to Koestler because, in *The Ghost in the Machine,* his position is once again (as in *The Sleepwalkers* and *The Act of Creation*) that of a latter-day Goethe; and, if one keeps in mind the basic duality implicit in *Faust,* many things about Koestler's arguments come into focus. For instance: it becomes clear why, in all three volumes, he gives the impression of producing not one but two or more books at the same time — books whose arguments have unfortunately not been disentangled. For this is just what he does. In each case, he leaves it to us to distinguish the *truths* he is explaining from the *Truth* he is preaching; and these are no more connected than Goethe's Organicist *Weltanschauung* was to the organicist methodology of Leibniz.

In the first volume, Koestler wrote perceptively and intelligently about the Renaissance astronomers, particularly Copernicus and Kepler; but he coupled these sensitive intellectual portraits with a grossly simplistic Message to the effect that scientists make theoretical discoveries by a blind, unreasoning Intuition — moving unwittingly through their problem-situations like sleepwalkers across a darkened room. In the second volume, he combined some ingenious psychological analogies between scientific discovery, artistic creation, and wit, with a grandiose scheme of biological and psychological "hierarchies" intended to "break the grip" of Mechanistic Determinism, and demonstrate the potential glory of man. In both cases some intriguing ideas, expressed with all Koestler's practiced literary skill, were presented as the basis of a revelatory message which had nothing to do with the case.

His new book continues the same pattern; only this time the display of "real science" is carried to extreme lengths. Koestler sets himself to demonstrate two things — first that, along with the "glory" of his artistic and scientific creativity, man inherits also a "predicament," in the form of a tendency to paranoia and self-destruction; and secondly, that, in the light of a properly balanced view of modern biology and psychology, this "paranoid streak in man which has made such an appalling mess of our history" can be seen to originate in our genetic make-up, to be corrected only by an "adaptive mutation."

Now if there really were adequate scientific grounds either for Koestler's diagnosis, or for his prescription, our species would indeed be in a tragic (and probably irremediable) situation. So we must look carefully both at the meaning Koestler attaches to his conclusion, and at the way he uses scientific material to support it. In the event, he gets around to the central thesis only in the final third of the book: the previous 220 pages comprise his preparatory survey of the natural sciences on whose testimony he intends to rely. He begins with psychology, and here he has some sound Leibnizian points to make. Whatever merit the idea of "reflexes" may have had in analyzing the operations of the autonomic nervous system, it was always a delusion to suppose that this category could be used to account for *all* human behavior—notably, linguistic and "language-mediated" behavior. True: this delusion is still active in parts of the American academic world, thanks to the influence of Watson and Skinner; though my own observation is that the Skinnerians are by now a self-isolated minority. More relevant is the fact that even Pavlov himself never supposed that the idea of "conditioned reflexes" could be extended to the higher mental functions of the central nervous system; and his successors in Russia, such as Vygotsky and Luria, have made good use of his complementary ideas about "signalling systems" and "rule-governed communication." (Curiously, Koestler makes the same mistake as the American psychologists he so dislikes, as his few scornful allusions to Pavlov indicate: he does not realize that the theory of "conditioned reflexes" was only the *first part* of Pavlov's physiological psychology, and one that he himself never imagined was adequate to cover the higher mental functions.)

If we adopt a more acceptable psychology, Koestler goes on to argue, we shall see that the understanding of human behavior calls for the idea of *rule-governed strategies;* and he hastens to apply the same idea to organic systems of every kind. At all levels, he claims, we must see the "directive behavior" of organs and organisms as exemplifying similar "strategies." The organic world is not a congeries of mechanisms but—to use his own neologisms—a "holarchy of holons": interacting systems whose individual operations must be understood in essentially teleological terms. This brings Koestler up against the subject which is the eternal stumbling-block for ideologues of all tendencies: organic evolution. For he cannot rest comfortably with the neo-Darwinian idea that, in themselves, the genetic mutations that occur in the germ-cells of animal populations are casually and functionally unrelated to the life-situations with which the resulting mutant individuals will have to cope. Such a belief undercuts the (teleological) idea of "strategies" at the point where he most needs it—i.e., at the intersection of biochemistry and history. Somehow or other, the biological evidence must be made to yield a notion of "mutations" which is less "random" and more "adaptive."

To this end, Koestler spends much of his second hundred pages citing authentic evidence of "adaptiveness" in the behavioral interactions between evolving populations and their environments, under the impression that, in this way, he can weaken the neo-Darwinian theory. Of course, he does nothing of the sort. All that neo-Darwinists rightly deny is that molecular changes in the ova and sperm of animals are (or could conceivably be) influenced *beforehand* by the future needs of their progeny's lives. Still, it is going to be important for Koestler's eventual thesis, to show if possible that "adaptiveness" is built into the operation of biological systems throughout history, and right down to the lowest level. Otherwise (if I get the point of his terminology) the "holons" will not form a true "holarchy." And how could this program be carried through if one conceded that the very material of organic evolution consisted of "blind, random mutations"?

So we arrive, finally, at Koestler's central topic. His account of our human "predicament" places the cause of human paranoia in an "imbalance" between different parts of the brain: specifically, in a "dissonance between the reactions of neocortex and limbic system." If we do not always act wisely and calmly, this is because our defective brains do not permit us to do so; and only an "adaptive mutation" will enable us to overcome this defect. Such a "mutation" will have to be produced at the molecular level by beneficent "biochemical engineering." If we are to avert the ultimate historical catastrophe, we must quickly develop a Pill (his capitalization) to bring about—or imitate—the necessary "mutation."

This conclusion—the climax of Koestler's argument throughout three long books—occupies only the final ten pages of *The Ghost in the Machine,* and I have read these pages several times with great care. I have to report that I can still find no real connection between Koestler's prescription for human folly and the "scientific evidence" he offers in its support. After all that has gone before, we expect, at least, a call for an "artificially-induced mutation" aimed at "improving" the functional balance between neocortex and limbic system in the brains of our offspring. Instead, Koestler calls merely for a new, superior tranquilizer or "mental stabiliser," with which we are to control our own brains, rather than change our children's. But why do we need all the preceding argument to prove what a drink or a phenobarb will demonstrate—that applied biochemistry can help to settle the nerves?

The points at issue in this book *appear* connected, only if one is committed beforehand to a teleological interpretation of organic evolution. At least three separate theses are involved, with two further sub-theses: (i) that the major evils in human history are consequences of a species-specific psychosis, rather than (as historians assume) a mixture of genuine conflicts of interest, miscalculations, and occasional neurotic fears; (ii) that this species-wide psychosis derives from an anatomical source in the inadequate control of the (rational) neocortex over the (paranoid) limbic system; and (iii) that such an anatomical inadequacy has parallels in the other "mistakes" of evolution—e.g., in some of the arthropods. To which one must add: (iv) the assumption that the contrast between rational and paranoid behavior has direct parallels at a neuroanatomical level *at all;* and (v) the belief that, if it were in fact clinically desirable to change the balance of action between neocortex and limbic system, this could be done in a sufficiently discriminating manner by pharmaceutical means alone.

Each of these five theses would take much more elaborate discussion to support than Koestler has room for; and none of them could, in the present state of things, be defended in any but the most tentative of spirits. In the event, Koestler's whole package hangs together only on account of item (iii). Here is where we run up against the central issue between Koestler's teleological world-picture and the current theories of organic evolution he finds so inadequate. For the very idea of "evolution" as "succeeding" or "making mistakes" takes for granted what is by now highly questionable: that the historical succession of organic forms can be properly interpreted as the outcome of a sequence of purposive "strategies." Without such an interpretation, indeed, what sense do phrases like "evolutionary mistake" have? Yet man is the first, and to the best of our knowledge the only, species which has *understood* its evolutionary situation well enough even to *try* to change its structure and mode of life in response to the demands of that situation; and, unless the idea of "trying to adapt" makes sense, how can the ideas of "succeeding" or "failing" possibly be applied either? It is perhaps no accident that, at this crucial point in his argument, the books to which Koestler turns for testimony and support were largely written (like Gaskell's *Origin of Vertebrates* of 1908) at a time when genetics scarcely existed as a science, and its application to the history of evolutionary change was at least twenty years away.

What has gone wrong? The answer is that Koestler is here repeating Goethe's mistake. As we have seen, his selection of scientific illustrations is intentionally tendentious: it is aimed (as he declares in the Preface) not to weigh up rival hypotheses, but to undercut an "image of man" as "a conditioned reflex-automaton produced by chance mutations...the antiquated slot-machine model based on the naively mechanistic world-view of the nineteenth century." This model he sees as still entrenched in "scientific orthodoxy" today; and we shall not achieve a balanced conception of our essential humanity unless we replace it by an alternative "holarchic" world-view, limiting the scope of mechanistic science with the help of the distinction between "organized holons" and "mere parts."

If however we insist on the distinction between Science as theoretical hypothesis and Science as the material for *Weltanschauungen*, it becomes possible to disentangle Koestler's message from its theoretical wrappings. It is—to make its theological character explicit —a Manichean or Zoroastrian message. Evolution has left man at the mercy of two contrary urges: a constructive one that works for good—this was the topic of *The Act of Creation*—and a self-destructive principle of evil that subverts the achievements of individuals and institutions alike. These antagonistic principles unite man to the universe, having been at work throughout cosmic history; and this insight restores the "meaning" which the "blind mutations" of neo-Darwinism took away from organic evolution. Man's hope of glory is thus balanced by his looming predicament—in the form of a genetical counterpart of original sin. Whereas Teilhard preached a bland doctrine of salvation through cosmic progress, Koestler is the profit of a harsher biological Calvinism: though he shares with Teilhard an all-embracing cosmic vision borrowed ultimately from Lamarck, he sternly insists that the final outcome of Evolution may well be Armageddon, or the Damnation of the Species.

I have good reasons for insisting that, in the last resort, Koestler's book must be considered not as science, but as theology. Scientifically, there is never sufficient reason for choosing one worldview rather than another; and there are usually good arguments for suspending judgment and declining the choice. If Koestler had written throughout in the spirit of Leibniz rather than Goethe—simply emphasizing the need to supplement "mechanicist" explanations of physiological structures by "organicist" analyses of the functions and activities of the systems concerned—things would then have been very different. The result might then have been to improve our understanding, but it would have led to no message. In that case, however, Koestler would have had to paint a different picture of contemporary science. For, after all, there is no such entrenched orthodoxy as he alleges; and he as good as admits this in an appendix, in which he excuses himself for "flogging dead horses." Now, as always, there are branches of biology and psychology—such as embryology and language-learning—whose theories depend on "integrative" concepts, just as there are others—such as molecular biology and reflexology—that are concerned with "reductionist" analyses. The kind of modest, rationally critical mileage being got *within* Science from Leibnizian concepts could be illustrated again and again from the former branches; we can, for instance, study the life-history of the cell, or the perception of colors, or the development of mental processes in children at all, only if we are prepared to accept cells, observers, and/or children as "monadic" units or agents to begin with.

Even so, an enthronement of "integrative" concepts within biological theory—i.e., a methodological victory for Leibnizian organicism over a one-sided Cartesian mechanism—would still fall
short of what Koestler's message requires. For that, what is needed
is a theological victory for Goethean Organicism over Mechanistic
Science of all varieties, with the entire historical process governed
throughout by the rival principles of good and evil. As Julian
Huxley found when he tried to argue against his grandfather, we
are (for all that Science can tell us) at liberty to view the cosmic-
process-as-a-whole in whatever light we please.

Those who defend a true humanism in a scientific age will do well
to re-read their Michel de Montaigne. All this to-do about "blind
mutations" and universal "urges" would have struck Montaigne
as terribly presumptuous. Who are we humans (he would ask) to
project our own ambitions onto the history of the universe? Among
historians of human affairs, this lesson was learned long ago: none
but the most naive Marxian and Christian historiographers still
see the Hand of God, or the Dialectic, in the detailed sequence of
temporal events. The same lesson will eventually get through to
our twentieth-century natural theologians also. For there is no
reason to see the history of Nature, either, as pregnant with a message; and it is human vanity, equally, to claim a basis in science for
an unquenchable evolutionary optimism like Teilhard's or Huxley's, or for a dark and romantic irrationalism.

P.S. After preparing this review I received a letter from Koestler's publisher:

Dear Reviewer:

On February 26 Macmillan will publish *The Ghost in the Machine*,
Arthur Koestler's first new book since *The Act of Creation* in 1964.

In this book Mr. Koestler proposes a pharmaceutical solution to
man's self-destructive urge: a pill to correct the streak of paranoia
inherent in a man which, in this post-Hiroshima age, must inevitably
lead to extermination.

The birth control pill can save man from outbreeding himself. The
pill which Arthur Koestler forsees can save man from genocide.

If there were such a pill—a "peace" pill—would you take it?

Publicity Director

Above the signature was glued a red, heart-shaped pellet. I have three comments: (1) Can an author of Koestler's experience *not know* what his publishers are doing in his name? This sort of publicity speaks for itself, since it uses the language of quackery, not of science. (2) The claims made for this imaginary pill are oddly like those Leary makes for LSD, and the arguments against them are the same—that a pharmaceutical millennium would only threaten our capacity for moral and intellectual judgment, and accelerate our return to the world of *Darkness at Noon*. (3) Finally: if there were such a pill, would Arthur Koestler take it?

Chronology of Important Dates

1905	Born in Budapest, September 5, the only child of solidly middle-class parents.
1922-26	Undergraduate science student at the University of Vienna; quit before obtaining degree.
1926-30	Traveled to Palestine to join Jabotinsky's "Zionist Activists" Movement; became disillusioned. Held various down-and-out jobs before becoming a correspondent for the Ullstein newspaper chain.
1930-32	Foreign editor, *B. Z. am Mittag,* and science editor, *Vossische Zeitung,* Berlin. Joined the German Communist party in December 1931.
1932	Quit Ullstein's; traveled in the Soviet Union.
1933-35	Worked off and on for Comintern Propaganda Office in Paris. Married Dorothy Asher in 1935 (separated 1937, divorced 1950).
1936	At outbreak of Spanish Civil War, traveled to Spain for the Comintern.
1937	During third trip to Spain, captured by Nationalist troops at Malaga, imprisoned and sentenced to death; freed after ninety-five days because of British press campaign on his behalf. Wrote and published *Spanish Testament* in London.
1938-40	In France, resigned from Communist party, wrote *Darkness at Noon.* Interned after Nazi invasion, escaped to Britain, recorded experiences in *Scum of the Earth.*
1941-42	Served in British Pioneer Corps. Published *Darkness at Noon;* rewrote *Spanish Testament* into *Dialogue with Death.*
1943-45	His novel *Arrival and Departure* greeted by laudatory reviews, especially in America. His essays, later collected in *The Yogi and the Commissar,* ignited political controversy.

1945-46   Traveled to Palestine; wrote pro-Zionist *Thieves in the Night;* later turned against Zionism in *Promise and Fulfillment* (1949).

1946-47   Publication in Paris of French edition of *Darkness at Noon* added to political controversy about Communism for France. Koestler in Paris answered all attacks.

1948   First visit to America; Koestler increasingly vocal in his anti-Communism.

1949   Published first science book, *Insight and Outlook.*

1950-51   Published memoir in *The God That Failed.* Traveled to America, gave anti-Communist lectures. Visiting Chubb Fellow, Yale University. Married Mamaine Paget (divorced 1953).

1952-54   Lived in America; wrote and published two volumes of memoirs, *Arrow in the Blue* (1952) and *The Invisible Writing* (1954).

1955   Announced in foreword to *Trail of the Dinosaur* that he would no longer write about politics.

1956   Active in campaign against capital punishment, published *Reflections on Hanging.*

1957-68   Increasing interest in mysticism, including a trip to the Orient, recorded in *The Lotus and the Robot* (1961), and in science, culminating in the publication of the trilogy, *The Sleepwalkers* (1959), *The Act of Creation* (1964), and *The Ghost in the Machine* (1968). Married Cynthia Jefferies, 1965.

1969-75   Continued work in mysticism and science; published books on ESP and biological theory. Named C.B.E. (Commander of the Order of the British Empire), 1972, and C. Lit. (Companion of Literature), 1974.

1976   Brought out thirtieth book in English, *The Thirteenth Tribe.*

Notes on the Editor and Contributors

MURRAY A. SPERBER, the editor of this volume, is also the editor of *And I Remember Spain: A Spanish Civil War Anthology* and the author of articles on modern literature and film. He is an assistant professor of English at Indiana University in Bloomington.

HENRY DAVID AIKEN, philosopher and educator, is the author of *The Age of Ideology, The Predicament of the University,* and many other works. He is the Charles Goldman Professor of Philosophy at Brandeis University, Waltham, Massachusetts.

A. J. AYER is best known for his seminal works on logical positivism, *The Foundations of Empirical Knowledge* and *Thinking and Meaning.* He was Grote Professor of Mind and Logic at the University of London, 1946-1959.

SAUL BELLOW, recipient of the 1976 Nobel Prize for Literature, is one of the most prolific American novelists *(The Adventures of Augie March, Herzog,* and *Humboldt's Gift,* among others). He has taught at a number of universities, most recently the University of Chicago.

MALCOLM COWLEY's writing career, primarily as an essayist and critic, has spanned almost half a century. His many books include *Exile's Return, The Literary Situation,* and his edition, *The Portable Faulkner.*

ISAAC DEUTSCHER was one of the most important political essayists and biographers of the century. His three-volume life of Trotsky is a touchstone of political biography.

WILLIAM EMPSON has written many volumes of poetry and literary criticism, including *Seven Types of Ambiguity* and *Some Versions of Pastoral.* He taught in China for many years and ended his academic career as professor of English literature, Sheffield University.

LESLIE FIEDLER, educator and literary *agent provocateur,* is the author of many works of literary and cultural criticism, including *An End to Innocence* and *Love and Death in the American Novel.* He teaches in the Department of English, State University of New York, Buffalo.

STUART HAMPSHIRE writes mainly about philosophy and politics. Among his books are *Freedom of Mind and Other Essays* and *Thought and Action*. He is warden of Wadham College, Oxford University.

F. O. MATTHIESSEN was probably the most distinguished American literary scholar of his generation. His *American Renaissance: Art and Expression in the Age of Emerson and Whitman* remains a central literary document. He taught at Harvard from 1929 until his death in 1950.

MAURICE MERLEAU-PONTY was one of the leading figures in the French philosophical movements of existentialism and phenomenology. Among his many publications were *Sense and Non-sense* and *Phenomenology and Perception*.

JAMES R. NEWMAN has written and edited many books on science, including *The Rule of Folly*.

GEORGE ORWELL is best known for his fictions *Animal Farm* and *1984* and his memoirs *Down and Out in Paris and London, The Road to Wigan Pier,* and *Homage to Catalonia*. But these books were only a small part of his writing, and much of his nonfiction has been collected in the four-volume *Collected Essays, Journalism, and Letters,* edited by Sonia Orwell and Ian Angus.

V. S. PRITCHETT's long career as a man of letters includes many volumes of fiction, criticism, and, most recently, memoirs *(A Cab at the Door)*. He was Beckman Professor at the University of California, Berkeley, 1962.

HAROLD ROSENBERG, art critic and cultural historican, is the author of a number of books, including *The Tradition of the New* and *The De-Definition of Art,* as well as of a regular column in *The New Yorker*. He is on the faculty of the University of Chicago.

ISAAC ROSENFELD was one of the most brilliant young critics of the 1940s and 1950s. Although he published some fiction, his *Age of Enormity: Life and Writing in the Forties and Fifties* remains his testament.

STEPHEN SPENDER began publishing poetry and criticism in the 1930s. Works like *The Still Centre* made his reputation, and he has solidified it with a steady output ever since. He is professor of English literature, University College, University of London.

GEORGE STEINER is one of the most prolific contemporary critics. Among his many publications are *The Death of Tragedy* and *Language and Silence*. He is a fellow of New Hall, Cambridge University.

STEPHEN TOULMIN has written extensively on philosophy and science. His works include *Foresight and Understanding: An Enquiry Into the Aims of Science* and *Human Understanding.* He is a professor of philosophy at the University of Chicago.

REBECCA WEST's career extends well over half a century. She has published many books of fiction, nonfiction, and criticism, among them *The Harsh Voice* and *The Meaning of Treason.*

EDMUND WILSON was probably the most erudite and wide-ranging American man of letters of the last several decades. Of all his works, *To the Finland Station* remains the most remarkable.

Selected Bibliography

Books by Arthur Koestler (first edition cited)

Spanish Testament. London: Victor Gallancz, for the Left Book Club, 1937.

The Gladiators. London: Jonathan Cape, 1939.

Darkness at Noon. London: Jonathan Cape, 1941.

Scum of the Earth. London: Jonathan Cape, 1941.

Dialogue with Death. New York: Macmillan & Co., 1942.

Arrival and Departure. London: Jonathan Cape, 1943.

Twilight Bar: An Escapade in Four Acts. London: Jonathan Cape, 1945.

The Yogi and the Commissar and Other Essays. London: Jonathan Cape, 1945.

Thieves in the Night: Chronicle of an Experiment. London: Macmillan & Co., 1946.

Promise and Fulfillment: Palestine, 1917-1949. London: Macmillan & Co., 1949.

Insight and Outlook: An Inquiry into the Common Foundations of Science, Art, and Social Ethics. London: Macmillan & Co., 1949.

Untitled Memoir in *The God That Failed,* edited by Richard Crossman. London: Hamish Hamilton Co., 1950.

The Age of Longing. London: Collins and Co., 1951.

Arrow in the Blue: The First Volume of an Autobiography, 1905-1931. London: Collins, with Hamish Hamilton Co., 1951

The Invisible Writing: The Second Volume of an Autobiography, 1932-1940. London: Collins, with Hamish Hamilton Co., 1954.

Trail of the Dinosaur and Other Essays. London: Collins and Co., 1955.

Reflections on Hanging. London: Victor Gollancz, 1957.

The Sleepwalkers: A History of Man's Changing Vision of the Universe. London: Hutchinson & Co., 1959.

The Lotus and the Robot. London: Hutchinson & Co., 1961.

Editor, *Suicide of a Nation? An Enquiry into the State of Britain Today* London: Hutchinson & Co., 1964.

The Act of Creation. London: Hutchinson & Co., 1964.

The Ghost in the Machine. London: Hutchinson & Co., 1968.

Drinkers of Infinity: Essays, 1955-1967. London: Hutchinson & Co., 1969.

Editor, with J. R. Smythies, *Beyond Reductionism: New Perspectives in the Life Sciences.* London: Hutchinson & Co., 1971.

The Case of the Mid-Wife Toad. London: Hutchinson & Co., 1972.

The Roots of Coincidence. London: Hutchinson & Co., 1972.

The Call Girls: A Tragi-Comedy with Prologue and Epilogue. London: Hutchinson & Co., 1973.

With Sir Alister Hardy and Robert Harvie, *The Challenge of Chance.* London: Hutchinson & Co., 1973.

The Heel of Achilles: Essays, 1968-1973. London: Hutchinson & Co., 1975.

The Thirteenth Tribe. London: Hutchinson & Co., 1976.

Books, Articles, and Reviews about Koestler

Atkins, John. *Arthur Koestler.* London: Constable & Co., 1956.

Benson, Frederic. "War of Ideas." In *Writers in Arms: The Literary Impact of the Spanish Civil War,* pp. 134-89. New York: New York University Press, 1967.

Birkenfeld, G. "Die Deutschen and Arthur Koestler," *Der Monat,* 1949; pp. 99-101.

Borkenau, Franz. "Yogi and Commissar," *Tribune* [London], May 11, 1945; p. 15.

Calder, Jenni. *Chronicles of Conscience: A Study of Arthur Koestler* and *George Orwell.* London: Martin Secker and Warburg Co., 1968.

Chiaromonte, Nicola. "Koestler or Tragedy Made Futile," *Politics,* September 1945; pp. 266-70.

Cowley, Malcolm. "Punishment and Crime," *New Republic,* June 2, 1941; pp. 766-67.

_____. "Decline and Fall," *New Republic,* December 8, 1941; pp. 768-69.

_____. "Port of Refuge," *New Republic,* November 22, 1943; pp. 721-22.

Crossman, R. H. S. Review of *The Age of Longing,* by Arthur Koestler. *New Statesman and Nation,* April 28, 1951; p. 482.

Davis, Robert Gorham. "The Sharp Horns of Koestler's Dilemma," *Antioch Review,* December 1944; pp. 503-17.

Handlin, Oscar. "The Worlds of Arthur Koestler," *Atlantic Monthly,* December 1968; pp. 92-96.

Harrington, Michael. "The Recurring Dilemma," *Commonweal,* January 6, 1956; pp. 359-60.

Harris, Harold, ed. *Astride the Two Cultures: Arthur Koestler at 70.* London: Hutchinson & Co., 1975.

Hausman, Carl R. "Understanding and the Act of Creation," *Review of Metaphysics,* September 1966; pp. 88-112.

Hicks, Granville. "Arthur Koestler and the Future of the Left," *Antioch Review,* June 1945; pp. 212-23.

Hobsbawm, Eric. "Koestler's England," *New York Review of Books,* April 2, 1964; pp. 13-14.

Hook, Sidney. "But There Was No Light," *New York Times Book Review,* March 5, 1961; pp. 7, 26.

Howe, Irving. "Malraux, Silone, and Koestler: The Twentieth Century." In *Politics and the Novel,* pp. 203-34. New York: Horizon Press, 1957.

Huber, Peter Alfred. *Arthur Koestler: Das literarische Werk.* Zurich: Freitz and Wasmuth Verlag, 1962.

Jovarsky, David. "The Head on Jung's Pillow," *New York Review of Books,* September 21, 1972; pp. 23-25.

Kahn, Louis. "Arthur Koestler: Dejudaicized Zionism." In *Mirrors of the Jewish Mind,* pp. 71-89. New York: Thomas Yoseloff and Co., 1968.

Klingopulus, G. D. "Arthur Koestler," *Scrutiny,* June 1949; pp. 82-92.

Laski, Harold J. "Mr. Koestler," *Manchester Guardian,* May 9, 1945; p. 3.

Martin, Kingsley. Review of *The Yogi and the Commissar,* by Arthur Koestler. *New Statesman and Nation,* September 22, 1945; pp. 197-98.

Medawar, P. B. "Koestler's Theory of the Creative Act," *New Statesman and Nation,* June 19, 1964; pp. 950-52.

Miller, Perry. "Koestler as Pedagogue," *Nation,* March 3, 1951; p. 207.

Mortimer, Raymond. "Arthur Koestler," *Cornhill Magazine,* Winter 1946; pp. 213-22.

Mudrick, Marvin. "Wooldridge, Koestler, and Watson: Prometheus at Work and Play." In *On Culture and Literature,* pp. 29-38. New York: Horizon Press, 1971.

Nedava, J. *Arthur Koestler.* London: Robert Anscombe and Co., 1948.

Niebuhr, Reinhold. "To Moscow—and Back," *Nation,* January 28, 1950; pp. 88-90.

_____. "Justice and the Death Penalty," *New Republic,* August 26, 1957; pp. 18-19.

Nott, Kathleen. "The Bloom and the Buzz," *Commentary,* November 1964; pp. 84-88.

Orwell, George. Review of *Darkness at Noon,* by Arthur Koestler, *New Statesman and Nation,* January 4, 1941; pp. 15-16.

_____. "Freud or Marx?" *Manchester Evening News,* December 9, 1943; p. 2.

_____. "Catastrophic Gradualism," [Written 1945; first published in *Commonwealth Review,* November 1945.] In *The Collected Essays, Journalism, and Letters of George Orwell,* edited by Sonia Orwell and Ian Angus, 4: 15-19. New York: Harcourt, Brace and World, 1968.

Padev, Michael. "The Invisible Complex," *Punch,* July 28, 1954, pp. 149-50.

Phillips, William. "Koestler and the Political Novel," *Nation,* August 26, 1944; pp. 241-42.

Pritchett, V. S. Review of *The Gladiators,* by Arthur Koestler. *Christian Science Monitor,* April 15, 1939; p. 10.

_____. Review of *The God That Failed,* ed. R. H. S. Crossman. *New Statesman and Nation,* January 21, 1950; p. 68.

———. Review of *Arrow in the Blue,* by Arthur Koestler. *New Statesman and Nation,* November 8, 1952; pp. 550-51.

Rahv, Philip. "Koestler and Homeless Radicalism." In *Image and Idea,* pp. 173-81. New York: New Directions, 1949.

Rovere, Richard. "A Matter of Life and Death," *New Yorker,* September 14, 1957; pp. 164-67.

Schlesinger, Arthur M., Jr. "Dim Views of the Red Star," *Saturday Review of Literature,* January 7, 1950; p. 11.

Shechner, Mark. Review of *The Thirteenth Tribe,* by Arthur Koestler. *Nation,* November 20, 1976; pp. 535-36.

Spender, Stephen. "Anatomy of a Hero," *Time and Tide,* January 1, 1944; pp. 11-13.

Strachey, John. "Koestler." In *The Strangled Cry,* pp. 1-23. London: Routledge & Kegan Paul, 1962.

Swingewood, Alan. "The Revolution Betrayed: Koestler and Serge." In *The Novel and Revolution,* pp. 169-89. London: Macmillan & Co., 1975.

Trilling, Diana. "Revolution and Neurosis," *Nation,* December 4, 1943; pp. 672-73.

———. Review of *Thieves in the Night,* by Arthur Koestler. *Nation,* November 9, 1946; pp. 530-34.

Toulmin, Stephen. "Koestler's Act of Creation: Vision, Theory, Romance," *Encounter,* July 1964; pp. 58-70.

"War of Nerves." *Times Literary Supplement,* April 20, 1951, p. 244.

Weintraub, Stanley. "The Adopted Englishman." In *The Last Great Cause: The Intellectuals and The Spanish Civil War,* pp. 120-43. New York: Weybright and Talley Co., 1968.

West, Anthony. "Some Conceptions of Man," *New Yorker,* March 17, 1951; pp. 121-22.

———. "Turns for the Worse," *New Yorker,* November 1, 1952; pp. 113-17.

Woodcock, George. "Arthur Koestler." In *The Writer and Politics,* pp. 147-83. London: Porcupine Press Co., 1947.

Woolf, Leonard. "The Promised Land," *New Statesman and Nation,* October 29, 1949; pp. 490-92.